DISCOVER

JESUS

AN ILLUSTRATED ADVENTURE FOR KIDS

DISCOVER JESUS

AN ILLUSTRATED ADVENTURE FOR KIDS

Tracy M. Sumner

SHILOH ! kidz
An Imprint of Barbour Publishing, Inc.

Interior layout design by Greg Jackson, Thinkpen Design

Published by Shiloh Kidz, an imprint of Barbour Publishing, Inc., 1810 Barbour Drive, Uhrichsville, Ohio 44683, www.shilohkidz.com

Our mission is to inspire the world with the life-changing message of the Bible.

 Member of the Evangelical Christian Publishers Association

Printed in China.

000237 0520 HA

CONTENTS

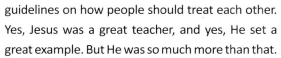

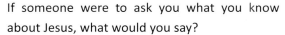

BEFORE YOU GET STARTED

If someone were to ask you what you know about Jesus, what would you say?

You probably know that Jesus was born a little over two thousand years ago in the land of Israel in a town called Bethlehem. And you probably know that He died on a cross so that people could be forgiven for their sins. Maybe you've heard some great stories about the miracles He performed, or even the important things He taught about loving God and other people.

That's a good start. But with this book, you have the opportunity to learn a lot more.

Walking on the water, Jesus rescues Peter—who'd been walking on water too until he took his eyes off the Lord.

Jesus was the greatest man who ever lived. He changed how people came to God for forgiveness for their sins. He taught incredible lessons about how to live—and He set the perfect example of living a good life. He performed miracles so that people could know that He was telling the truth when He said that God had sent Him.

Some people believe that Jesus was just an unusually good man who left behind some guidelines on how people should treat each other. Yes, Jesus was a great teacher, and yes, He set a great example. But He was so much more than that.

The Bible calls Jesus "Immanuel," which means "God with us" (Matthew 1:23). That means that God Himself had come to earth! He was the only human being ever to follow every one of the Old Testament rules for living—what many call "the Law." He was the Savior who would take the punishment for people's sins by dying on a cross—and then be raised back to life. He is the one and only way people can come to God and live forever with Him.

Throughout history, lots of people have started religions. But Jesus was different from any other religious figure. For one thing, centuries before He came to the world, prophets predicted many things about Jesus—and they all came true! Also, Jesus didn't just claim to be sent from God. . .He claimed to be *God in a human body*. And He is the only religious figure to defeat death. God the Father brought Jesus back to life after His terrible death on a cross.

Jesus "has bought men for God from every family and from every language and from every kind of people and from every nation" (Revelation 5:9).

7

All the things you've just read about Jesus are recorded in the pages of the Bible. In this book, you'll learn about these things and many, many more, such as:

- The reason Jesus came to earth in the first place.
- "Prophecies"—things men who loved God and listened to Him said about Jesus long before He was born.
- The land of Israel when Jesus came to earth.
- Jesus' miraculous birth in Bethlehem.
- Jesus' life as a boy in the land of Israel.
- The incredible things Jesus did and said when He was on earth.
- Jesus' arrest, trial, and death on the cross. . . and how God raised Him from the dead.
- The start of "the church"—meaning all the people who believe in Jesus and follow Him.
- The amazing things Jesus' followers did after He had returned to heaven.

Each of the chapters in this book includes important stories and facts about Jesus. Each chapter also includes some interesting features having to do with that chapter's main topic:

- **"It's in the Bible!":** Verses related to the subject you're reading about.
- **"Who said that?":** Things people said or wrote in the Bible, and a quick profile of that person.
- **"What does that mean?":** Words and phrases describing truths from the Bible and what they really mean.
- **"What does that mean to me?":** Important verses and how they apply to your faith in Jesus.

This book doesn't include everything Jesus did and said while He was on earth, or everything that other people wrote about Him in scripture. To learn everything about Jesus, you'll need to crack open your Bible and start reading for yourself—and I hope you will.

By the time you finish reading this book, though, you'll probably know some things about Jesus you didn't know before. And you may find it easier to answer your friends and family members when they ask you about Jesus!

Tracy M. Sumner
February 2019

Friends lower a paralyzed man down through the ceiling, seeking a healing from Jesus. You can read the whole story in Mark 2:1–12.

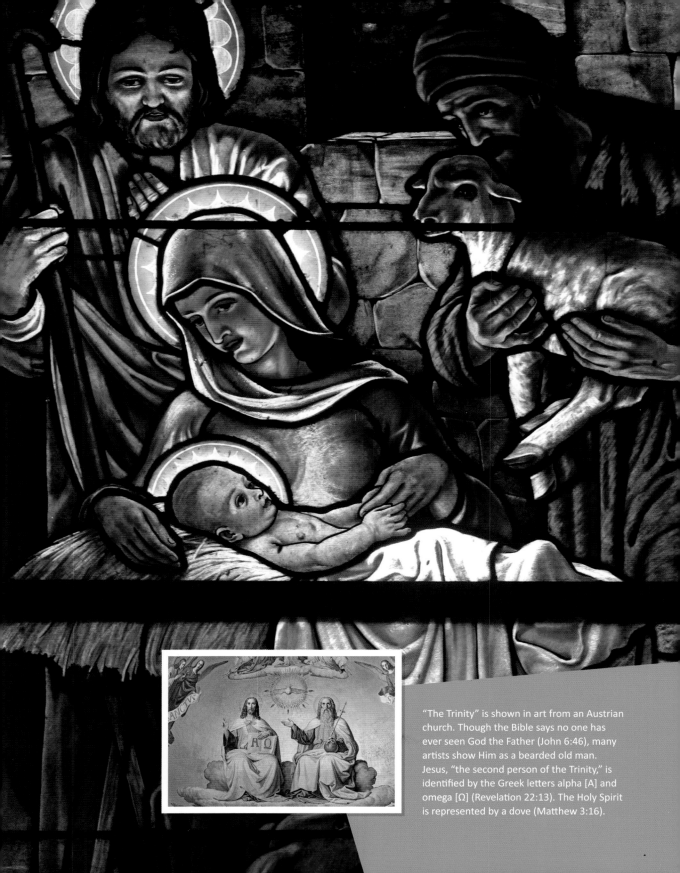

"The Trinity" is shown in art from an Austrian church. Though the Bible says no one has ever seen God the Father (John 6:46), many artists show Him as a bearded old man. Jesus, "the second person of the Trinity," is identified by the Greek letters alpha [A] and omega [Ω] (Revelation 22:13). The Holy Spirit is represented by a dove (Matthew 3:16).

At God's invitation, Abraham looks at the stars—an indication of how many descendants he would have some day.

Here's how that happened: There was a man named Abram who lived in a place called Haran; that was located in what is now the country of Iraq. One day, around 1900 BC, God told Abram to gather his family members, pack up his belongings, leave his home in Haran, and travel to a place he would be shown. God promised Abram that he and his family would be blessed and that they would become famous. God also promised Abram that everyone on earth, no matter where they lived, would benefit if he did what he was told:

Now the Lord said to Abram, "Leave your country, your family and your father's house, and go to the land that I will show you. And I will make you a great nation. I will bring good to you. I will make your name great, so you will be honored. I will bring good to

those who are good to you. And I will curse those who curse you. Good will come to all the families of the earth because of you."
GENESIS 12:1–3

The Bible doesn't say that Abram asked God any questions. He didn't ask where he was going or how long it would take to get there. Abram, his wife Sarai, his nephew Lot, and all their family members just packed up and hit the road. Eventually, they settled in a place called Canaan, the areas of modern-day Lebanon, Syria, Jordan, and Israel. It was a beautiful place with lots of land that produced crops for farmers who lived there. It would be a great place for Abram and his family to live!

One night, years after Abram had settled in Canaan, he was resting in his tent when God appeared. The Lord said He would protect Abram and reward him for his faithfulness. But Abram's first thought was of an heir—someone to give his money and things to when he died. In those days, men all wanted to have children so there would be someone to carry on the family name.

Abram and Sarai were older than this elderly Jewish couple—which would have made starting a family quite difficult. But nothing is too hard for God!

But Abram knew there was a problem attached to God's promise: he had no children! Even worse, Abram and Sarai were too old to start having kids. So Abram told God that he would make a servant named Eliezer the heir of all he owned. But God had another plan:

Then the word of the Lord came to him, saying, "This man will not be given what is yours. But he who will come from your own body will be given what is yours." He took him outside and said, "Now look up into the heavens and add up the stars, if you are able to number them." Then He said to him, "Your children and your children's children will be as many as the stars."
GENESIS 15:4–5

And God kept that promise.

WHAT DOES THAT MEAN TO ME?

Then Abram believed in the Lord, and that made him right with God (Genesis 15:6).

One of the most important parts of the message of salvation through Jesus is that we are saved through faith in Him. That means that God sees us as right with Him when we tell Him we believe what He has said—that Jesus came to live on earth and then die so our sins could be forgiven.

Jewish people—descendants of Abraham—crowd the Western Wall in Jerusalem. Abraham is also called the "father" of all people who follow God by faith in Jesus.

To remind Abram of this promise, God started calling him "Abraham," which means "father of many." And God changed Sarai's name to Sarah.

Though Abraham and Sarah were both very old by this time—and Sarah had never been able to become pregnant—God miraculously gave them a son. They named him Isaac.

After Isaac grew up, he married a woman named Rebekah. They were unable to have children for a long time also, but God again performed a miracle and gave them twin sons, one who was named Jacob.

Many years later, God gave Jacob this promise: "Your descendants will be as numerous as the dust of the earth! They will spread out in all directions—to the west and the east, to the north and the south. And all the families of the earth will be blessed through you and your descendants" (Genesis 28:14 NLT).

An old postage stamp highlights the "twelve tribes of Israel." Look up Genesis 49 and try to match each tribe with its image.

Does that promise sound familiar? If so, that's because it's basically the same thing God had promised Jacob's grandfather, Abraham. Even though Abraham and Sarah had just one son together, their grandson Jacob had *twelve* sons, and the families of each of those twelve sons grew in number to become a large group of people called a "tribe." Since God at one point changed Jacob's name to Israel (Genesis 32:28), these family groups came to be known as "the Twelve Tribes of Israel." Each of them was important for a different reason. For example, the nation of Israel's priests came from the tribe of Levi, Jacob's third son. The kings all came from the tribe of Judah, Jacob's fourth son.

The Bible says Jesus came from the tribe of Judah. You can read about that in Matthew 1:1–16 and Luke 3:23–38, which are Jesus' family records, also called His "genealogy." In Revelation, the last book of the New Testament, Jesus is called "the Lion of the Tribe of Judah" (5:5 NLT).

WHO SAID THAT?

"You intended to harm me, but God intended it all for good. He brought me to this position so I could save the lives of many people" (Genesis 50:20 NLT).

Joseph said these words to his brothers, who had sold him into slavery. Joseph wanted them to know that he would not seek to punish them because God had used the situation to ensure the survival of the people of Israel.

Jacob's second-youngest son, Joseph, played a huge role in the history of God's chosen nation, Israel. But for a long time, it didn't look like Joseph would be important at all.

Because he was Jacob's favorite, Joseph's brothers didn't like him very much. One day the brothers, in a fit of jealousy, sold Joseph to be a slave! He was carted off to Egypt, where he had to work for other people (and even spent time in jail for a crime he didn't commit). But eventually, miraculously, he became one of the most powerful men in the nation. As it turned out, God used the very thing Joseph's brothers had done to harm him to save the people of Israel from starvation. When God did that, He kept His plan on track for the salvation of people around the world.

Isn't it amazing? God used events long before Jesus came to earth to complete His plan of bringing the Savior into the world. When you read Genesis, you see how good God is, how much He loves you, and how He was working from the very beginning of time to make a way for you to spend eternity in heaven with Him.

Now that we've made our way through the book of Genesis, let's take a look at how God continued working out the plan of salvation through the rest of the Old Testament.

Joseph, great-grandson of Abraham, keeps his family—and God's plan for a Savior—alive during a famine.

THE FIRST BOOK OF MOSES

GENESIS.

God created the heaven

was without form, and
ss was upon the face of
he Spirit of God moved
d waters.

d, Let there be light: and

the light, that it was good
d the light from the

lesser ligh
stars also.

17 And
of the hea

18 And
the night

darkness

19 And
were th

20 An
forth

that ha
the ear

21 An
every
the wa

CHAPTER 2

THE OLD TESTAMENT: IT'S ALL ABOUT JESUS

IN THIS CHAPTER:

- How God protected His chosen people
- Old Testament sacrifices and what they had to do with Jesus
- When God had to discipline His people
- Old Testament prophecies about Jesus

When you think about which books of the Bible would tell you about Jesus, your thoughts probably go to the four Gospels—Matthew, Mark, Luke, and John—and the rest of the New Testament. But did you know that when you read the *Old Testament*, you're actually reading about Jesus? It's true! Even though Jesus' name isn't mentioned once in the Old Testament, those Bible books tell us a lot about Him.

You probably already know many of the cool stories from Old Testament. We've looked at the story of Adam and Eve and the account of Abraham, including God's promise to work through his descendants to bless many people throughout history.

After disobeying God, Adam and Eve are forced out of their home in the Garden of Eden. Their lives would be hard and they would ultimately die, but Adam and Eve could take courage in God's promise that one of their descendants would someday give birth to a Savior.

But these are more than just great stories. They're part of God's plan to bring Jesus into the world so He could teach and heal people, and then make forgiveness possible for everyone who has ever done wrong. That is, everyone!

In this chapter, we'll pick up where we left off in Chapter 1. Remember, God had called Abraham to leave his home in Haran and travel to a land he didn't even know about. That land, Canaan, was where God's people would live while He worked through one generation after another to prepare the world for Jesus' arrival.

But God didn't do this work in secret. He told many men about the coming of the Messiah, which is another name for Jesus Christ. These men are called "prophets," and they had a lot to say about Jesus, even though He would not arrive on earth for many centuries.

So keep reading. . .and prepare to be amazed. God did awesome things to make sure you could know Him and be a part of His plan for forgiveness and salvation.

A SAD LIFE IN EGYPT

Let's pick up the story of God's chosen people with Jacob's son Joseph, who became such an important person in Egypt.

Jacob and his family were living in Canaan when they suffered through a time of famine— that is, the people didn't have enough food for themselves or their animals. They were starving, so Jacob and seventy of his family members left Canaan and traveled to Egypt, where there was plenty of food to go around.

At first, the Egyptians welcomed the Israelites into their land. For many years after that, the people of Israel lived in peace with their new neighbors. But as more and more Israelites were being born (some people think as many as three million Israelites lived in Egypt at one time), the Egyptians began to worry that the Israelites might become too strong and take over the country.

To solve that "problem," Pharaoh (the ruler in Egypt) ordered that the Israelites work as slaves in Egypt. That was how it would be for the next four hundred years. Jacob's descendants built cities and roads for Pharaoh, who thought that if he worked the people hard enough, they would be too tired to have more children.

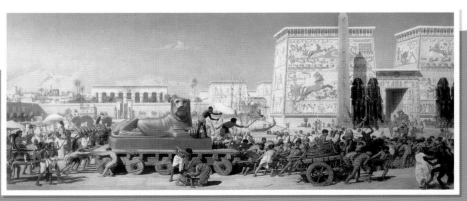

Israelites are forced to work on the Pharaoh's construction projects in Egypt.

From a burning bush, God called Moses to lead the people of Israel into the Promised Land—where the plan of salvation from sin would continue to move forward.

HEADING HOME TO CANAAN

The people of Israel weren't happy living as slaves. They worked very hard every day for no pay, and the Egyptians treated them terribly. The people cried out to God about their treatment, and God heard them. He sent a leader to free them from Egyptian slavery and guide them in their travel back to their homeland—which was His plan all along.

Around 1450 BC, God called a man named Moses to lead the Israelites out of Egypt. Moses was a shepherd who lived with his wife and her family in a placed called Midian. The Bible says Moses had grown up in Egypt, but had to run away to Midian after he killed an Egyptian for beating one of his fellow Hebrews. When Pharaoh found out what Moses had done, he ordered him killed for his crime.

Since he was a wanted man in Egypt, Moses stayed in Midian for forty years, working for his father-in-law. But he never forgot the suffering of his people back in Egypt. He wanted them to be free like he was. And God would call Moses to do something about that suffering.

One day, Moses was just doing the things shepherds do when God spoke to him about leading the people out of Egypt. In the wilderness at Mount Sinai, which the Bible calls "the mountain of God," Moses saw something strange: a bush that was on fire but wasn't burned up!

At first, he probably rubbed his eyes and looked twice to make sure he wasn't just seeing things. But then a voice spoke from the bush—the voice of God! "Moses, Moses!" God called out. When Moses answered, God said, "Do not come near. Take your shoes off your feet. For the place where you are standing is holy ground" (Exodus 3:4–5).

prophets what He was doing, and they shared His message with the world. When the people of Jesus' day saw His life and teaching and death on the cross, God wanted them to know for sure that He was the One sent to bring salvation to the world.

Some experts say that there are more than 125 predictions of the coming Savior in the Old Testament. That includes more than three thousand Bible verses! The Old Testament foretold (that is, told ahead of time) everything from Jesus' birth to His resurrection from the dead.

Clearly, God used the Old Testament to say something about His plan for forgiving sins!

THE OLD TESTAMENT PROPHETS

Ezekiel

Haggai

Hosea

Jeremiah

Habakkuk

Zechariah

Malachi

Micah

Joel

Isaiah

Nahum

Jonah

Daniel

Daniel

Obadiah

Amos

The prophet Micah spoke to both Israel and Judah, the northern and southern Jewish nations. He predicted that the Messiah, Jesus, would be born in Bethlehem (Micah 5:2).

WHAT THE PROPHETS SAID

The Old Testament tells the stories of many people who spoke or wrote prophecies that God had given them. The word *prophecy* means a message straight from God, and the word *prophet* refers to the person God chose to speak His words to the people.

God called a lot of prophets during Old Testament times. Men such as Samuel, Elijah, Elisha, David, and many others *spoke* the messages God had given them. But there were other prophets God used to *write down* messages that became books of the Bible. The first of these books, as it appears in your Bible, is Isaiah. It's part of a group (Jeremiah, Lamentations, Ezekiel, and Daniel are the others) called the "major prophets." Daniel is followed by twelve books called "minor prophets"—in order, they are Hosea, Joel, Amos, Obadiah, Jonah, Micah, Nahum, Habakkuk, Zephaniah, Haggai, Zechariah, and Malachi. "Minor" doesn't mean these books are less important but simply that they are shorter than others.

So how did the Old Testament prophets get the messages God wanted them to share? Centuries after the last of these prophets

WHO SAID THAT?

"Brothers, I know you and your leaders did this without knowing what you were doing. In this way, God did what He said He would do through all the early preachers. He said that Christ must suffer many hard things" (Acts 3:17–18).

The apostle Peter spoke these words to the people of Jerusalem after Jesus had died, been raised from the dead, and returned to heaven. He wanted them to understand that Jesus' suffering and death were the fulfillment of God's Old Testament promises of the Messiah.

preached to God's people, Jesus' disciple Peter explained it this way: "No part of the Holy Writings came long ago because of what man wanted to write. But holy men who belonged to God spoke what the Holy Spirit told them" (2 Peter 1:21). That means that the Old Testament prophecies about Jesus came straight from the heart and mind of God!

The Old Testament prophets preached their messages mostly to Israel and Judah, but a few of them wrote to other countries. Most of the time, the people didn't like what the prophets said. They hated being told that they needed to turn to God or else face His punishment for their sins. They often treated the prophets badly, even though their preaching included a message of hope for the people if they turned back to God.

The prophets' most hopeful message was God's promise to one day send the nation of Israel a Messiah. The word *Messiah* means the same thing as "Christ"—it refers to God's Chosen One, the Savior. You can find the idea in Psalm 2:2, which says, "The kings of the earth stand in a line ready to fight, and all the leaders are against the Lord and against His Chosen One."

Many prophecies about the coming Messiah are very detailed and specific. That was so people could see those prophecies fulfilled in the things Jesus did and said. Then they could believe that He was the Savior God had sent to the world.

This book can't discuss every single prophecy about Jesus. But let's take a look at some things God's prophets wrote and said about the Chosen One's birth, life, death, and resurrection.

JESUS' BIRTH

You probably already know the basics about Jesus' birth—after all, you hear them every year around Christmastime! We'll get into the details of that amazing event in Chapter 4. But in the meantime, did you know that centuries before Jesus' birth, Old Testament prophets wrote some amazing predictions about *how* it would happen? Here are some examples:

- Jesus would be from the family tree of King David (Jeremiah 23:5–6).
- His mother would be a woman who had never been with a man (Isaiah 7:14).
- He would be born in a city called Bethlehem of Judah (Micah 5:2).
- He would be born as a baby like everyone else, and He would be called "Wonderful Counselor," "Mighty God," "Everlasting Father," and "Prince of Peace." He would also possess a kingdom that would last forever (Isaiah 9:6–7 NLT).

- Many babies would die around the time of Jesus' birth (Jeremiah 31:15). This happened when the evil King Herod, jealous after hearing about a newborn "King of the Jews," ordered all young male children killed in an attempt to make sure *he* remained king.

Jesus' mother was a young woman named Mary. His birth was a miracle, since she had never been with a man. God caused Jesus to grow inside her.

JESUS' WORK HERE ON EARTH

When Jesus was about thirty years old, He started traveling around Israel (called "Palestine" at the time), teaching, preaching, and caring for people by doing incredible miracles. God had shown Old Testament prophets many of the great things Jesus would do while He was alive on earth. Here are some things the prophets told about what is called Jesus' "earthly ministry":

- A man (John the Baptist) would appear before Jesus' ministry started, to prepare people for Him (Isaiah 40:3–4).
- He would start His work in a place called Galilee (Isaiah 9:1–2).
- He would perform miracles of healing (Isaiah 35:5–6)
- He would teach the people of Israel how to live in a way that pleases God (Psalm 40:9).
- He would teach by telling stories called parables (Psalm 78:1–2).

- People would not listen to His parables or understand them (Isaiah 6:9–10).
- He would be humbled so that He could serve people (Psalm 8:5–6).
- He would bring good news and set people free (Isaiah 61:1)

WHO SAID THAT?

But He was hurt for our wrong-doing. He was crushed for our sins. He was punished so we would have peace. He was beaten so we would be healed (Isaiah 53:5).

The prophet Isaiah wrote these words about the coming Messiah, Jesus, who would come to earth to die a painful death on the cross so that your sins could be forgiven.

Jesus heals a blind man by touching His eyes with spit on His fingers. You can read the whole story in Mark 8:22–26.

JESUS' DEATH AND RESURRECTION

All during His time on earth, Jesus knew that His most important mission was to die and then be raised from the dead, so that people could be forgiven for their sins. Old Testament prophets included an amazing number of details about Jesus' death on the cross—as well as His resurrection. Here are some great examples:

- Jesus would be a humble man who rode into Jerusalem on a donkey colt, bringing salvation to all the world. People would be happy when He arrived (Zechariah 9:9–10).
- He would be betrayed for thirty pieces of silver (Zechariah 11:12–13).
- His closest friends would abandon Him (Psalm 31:11).
- He would be ridiculed and mistreated (Isaiah 50:3–6).
- People would reject Him and He would suffer (Isaiah 53:3).
- He would be wounded for our rebellion against God and die for our sin. He would be beaten so that we could be healed (Isaiah 53:5).
- He would be forsaken (that is, left alone) by God (Psalm 22:1).
- He would die alongside sinners but be buried with rich people (Isaiah 53:9).
- His body would not rot in a tomb, but God the Father would raise Him from the dead (Psalm 16:10).
- He would come back to earth from heaven as the Son of Man (Daniel 7:13–14).

- The people of Israel would one day realize that Jesus, the one they rejected and crucified, was their Messiah (Zechariah 12:10).

So there you have it! The Old Testament is more than a collection of great stories and wise instructions for how to live. It's also the story of how God used people and events—some good, some bad—to prepare the world for the arrival of the Savior, Jesus Christ.

Jesus carries His own cross to the execution site. The crucifixion is a terribly sad story—but it's followed by the joy of Jesus' resurrection!

WHEN GOD STOPPED TALKING

Many centuries after the Old Testament prophets told people about Jesus, the apostle Paul wrote, "But at the right time, God sent His Son. A woman gave birth to Him under the Law" (Galatians 4:4). That means that God had chosen the specific time that Jesus would come to earth, fulfilling the prophecies made about Him.

The last Old Testament book, Malachi, was written about 430 years before Jesus was born. During those years, the prophecies about Jesus stopped.

In Malachi's time, the Jewish people had returned to the land of Israel after spending seventy years in captivity in Babylon. After Babylon, a world power called the Persian Empire ruled over Israel. The Persians allowed the temple in Jerusalem, which had been destroyed by the Babylonians, to be rebuilt. For a while, the Jewish people could follow God's laws in their homeland.

But then the land and people of Israel came under the control of other nations. In 332 BC, a Greek king named Alexander the Great conquered the Persian Empire. Greece made the land of Israel into a province for almost two centuries, and some rulers tried to force the Jews to live and worship like Greeks. That led to a period of war called the Maccabean revolt in 142 BC, which left the people of Israel more free from outside rule. But that changed again in 63 BC, when the Roman Empire took control of Israel.

In the years just before Jesus' birth, the Jewish people in the land longed for God to fulfill His promises for a Messiah. They wanted someone to free them from the rule of outside kings and armies. That wasn't exactly God's plan—His Messiah would free people from their sins. But the time was now right. God worked through several individuals who loved Him and listened to His instructions to finally bring Jesus to the world.

Caesar Augustus ruled the Roman empire—including the biblical land of Israel—when Jesus was born in Judea.

The apostle Paul said Jesus came to earth "at the right time" (Galatians 4:4). Many people believe the rule of Rome was part of that—there was peace in the world and a road system that made it easier to spread the message of the Gospel.

PART II

WHEN GOD CAME TO EARTH

The story of Jesus' life on earth is told in the first four books of the New Testament—Matthew, Mark, Luke, and John. These books are called the "Gospels," and *Gospel* means "good news." The Gospels tell us about Jesus' birth, His work here on earth (what many people call His "earthly ministry"), and His death and resurrection.

If you've ever read through the four Gospels (and if you haven't, you should!), it might seem like they sometimes tell different stories. Well, the four Gospel writers all tell the same story, but they tell it in different ways and from different perspectives. Some writers included details the others left out, and the stories about Jesus' life are not always in the same order. For example, only Matthew and Luke tell us the story of Jesus' birth, and the two books focus on different details of that important event.

One reason the four Gospels are so different is that the authors were writing to different audiences. Matthew, for example, was written to Jewish readers, so it highlights Jesus' family tree (His genealogy) and mentions many Old Testament references to the coming Messiah. That way, Matthew's readers could see that Jesus was the long-awaited Messiah they had read about in the Old Testament.

The writer of Mark was not one of Jesus' twelve closest followers (also known as "apostles"), but he had followed Jesus. Mark wrote his book to non-Jewish readers, so he left out the genealogy and the Old Testament references Matthew had included. The third Gospel was addressed to someone named Theophilus, and Luke included many details not found in the others. Luke was the only non-Jewish writer of New Testament books (he also wrote Acts), so his books helped Gentile readers understand who Jesus was and what He means.

John, who was one of Jesus' twelve original apostles, wrote the fourth Gospel. This one is very different from the other three because it focuses more on the fact that Jesus was God in the flesh and that He had existed with God in eternity past. John includes many of Jesus' statements about who He really was and what that meant to people who heard Him speak.

In the next five chapters, you'll read some of the "highlights" of Jesus' time on this earth—including His birth, His childhood, His work, and His death and resurrection—as they appear in the four Gospels.

CHAPTER 3

THE REAL CHRISTMAS STORY

IN THIS CHAPTER:

- Angels visit Mary and Elizabeth
- The birth of John the Baptist
- Mary and Joseph travel to Bethlehem
- The birth of the Savior
- Shepherds visit the baby Jesus

If you asked most people what they like about Christmas, *gifts* would probably be near the top of their lists. Giving Christmas presents to people you care about is a lot of fun, and of course receiving them is great too!

What do you think would be the perfect Christmas gift? Would it be something you really need? Or do you like receiving things that are just fun to have?

There was one *perfect* Christmas gift, and it was given on the very first Christmas more than two thousand years ago. That was when God sent His only Son, Jesus, to be born in a little town called Bethlehem. After Jesus had grown up and started preaching, teaching, and performing miracles, He put it like this: "For God so loved the world that He gave His only Son. Whoever puts his trust in God's Son will not be lost but will have life that lasts forever" (John 3:16).

The best gifts are the ones we give out of love. There's no greater love than the love God has for us people—and there's no greater gift than the One He gave in the form of the man Jesus.

You can read the story of Jesus' birth in Matthew 1:18–2:2 and Luke 1:5–2:20. As you read those Bible passages, you'll also learn about the birth of John the Baptist, who "prepared the way" for Jesus. The Christmas story includes some great promises, several amazing miracles, and angels sharing God's message that the time had come for the Savior's birth.

Christmas gifts are lots of fun—but God's gift of Jesus changes lives forever.

like you do! She also knew it wasn't possible for her to have a baby. She had never been with a man in that way. So Mary asked the angel how she could have a baby.

The angel explained that God would do an amazing miracle, causing her to become pregnant with Jesus. He also told Mary that her child would be holy, and called the Son of God. Finally, the angel told Mary that her relative Elizabeth would be having her miracle baby in another three months. Mary may have still wondered what God was doing, but she decided to trust Him. She told Gabriel, "I am the Lord's servant. May everything you have said about me come true" (Luke 1:38 NLT).

Relatives Elizabeth (left) and Mary (right) meet to discuss their miraculous pregnancies—Elizabeth was too old to have children and Mary was carrying God's own Son, Jesus.

WHAT DOES THIS MEAN TO ME?

INCARNATION

When you hear your pastor or someone else who knows fancy terms about the Bible use the word *incarnation*, they're talking about God becoming fully human in the person of Jesus Christ. He actually lived on earth among sinful and needy people! John 1:14 puts it this way: "Christ became human flesh and lived among us."

A few days after the angel's visit, Mary left Joseph, her friends, and family behind and traveled to Jerusalem to see Elizabeth. Elizabeth was very happy to see Mary, and the baby still growing inside her leapt. At that moment, the Holy Spirit revealed to Elizabeth who Mary's baby was—the Messiah! She was so excited that she cried out to Mary:

"You are honored among women! Your Child is honored! Why has this happened to me? Why has the mother of my Lord come to me? As soon as I heard your voice, the baby in my body moved for joy. You are happy because you believed. Everything will happen as the Lord told you it would happen."
LUKE 1:42–45

The Gospel of Luke says that Mary stayed with Elizabeth for three months before she returned home to Nazareth. Many believe Mary helped Elizabeth when John was born. Meanwhile, though, Mary's fiancé Joseph was worried—and maybe heartbroken—when he found out that Mary was expecting a baby too.

IT'S IN THE BIBLE!

MARY'S SONG OF PRAISE (LUKE 1:46–55 NLT)

After Elizabeth spoke a blessing to Mary, the mother of Jesus responded with a song of praise called "The Magnificat." Here's how it begins:

"Oh, how my soul praises the Lord. How my spirit rejoices in God my Savior! For he took notice of his lowly servant girl, and from now on all generations will call me blessed. For the Mighty One is holy, and he has done great things for me."

Mary's husband-to-be, Joseph, had a job as a carpenter. One time, when Jesus' neighbors doubted His authority to teach, they asked, "Is not this the carpenter's son?" (Matthew 13:55).

Joseph loved God and lived the way God wanted him to live. But he and Mary were not yet married, and he knew he was not the father of the child Mary was expecting. Joseph decided to break their engagement, but he wanted to deal with Mary kindly. He planned to end their relationship privately so she wouldn't be embarrassed in public.

But before Joseph could do this, an angel from God appeared to him in a dream. "Joseph, son of David," the angel said, "do not be afraid to take Mary as your wife. She is to become a mother by the Holy Spirit. A Son will be born to her. You will give Him the name Jesus because He will save His people from the punishment of their sins" (Matthew 1:20–21).

When Joseph woke up from his dream, he knew what God wanted him to do. What had happened was an amazing blessing to him as well as to Mary, so he did not break his engagement. Instead, Joseph married her and later raised Jesus as his own son.

TRAVELING TO BETHLEHEM (LUKE 2:1–20)

Before Jesus was born, Mary and Joseph lived in Nazareth in Galilee. That part of the world was controlled by the Roman Empire. Just before Jesus' birth, Emperor Augustus (who ruled from 27 BC until his death in AD 14), wanted a count of everyone in the empire so the Roman government could make sure they were paying their taxes. Augustus ordered everyone to return to the town where their families originated to register their names.

Joseph was a descendant of King David, so he and Mary traveled about seventy miles from Nazareth to Bethlehem (also known as the City of David) in Judea. Many other people had also journeyed to Bethlehem for the census, so Mary and Joseph couldn't find a place to stay the night. Every house was full and every bed taken, so they ended up in a stable—a place where people kept their animals! It wasn't a warm room with clean bedding, and it probably didn't smell very good. . .but it was better than sleeping outside.

That night, Mary's special baby was born. Back then, newborns were usually wrapped in a long, soft cloth called "swaddling clothes." Mary and Joseph wrapped the baby Jesus in the cloth to keep Him warm. Then they laid Him in a manger, a food box for cows.

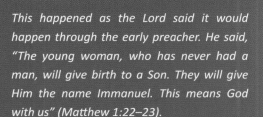

WHO SAID THAT?

This happened as the Lord said it would happen through the early preacher. He said, "The young woman, who has never had a man, will give birth to a Son. They will give Him the name Immanuel. This means God with us" (Matthew 1:22–23).

These words were recorded by the Old Testament prophet Isaiah in his book of prophecy (Isaiah 7:14). The apostle Matthew, one of the twelve men who followed Jesus during His ministry here on earth, quoted Isaiah in his Gospel. Matthew wanted people to know that Mary's pregnancy with Jesus—even though she had never been with a man—was the fulfillment of Isaiah's prophecy.

This old Roman coin shows an image of Caesar Augustus—the ruler who demanded that everyone return to their family's hometowns to be counted—and taxed.

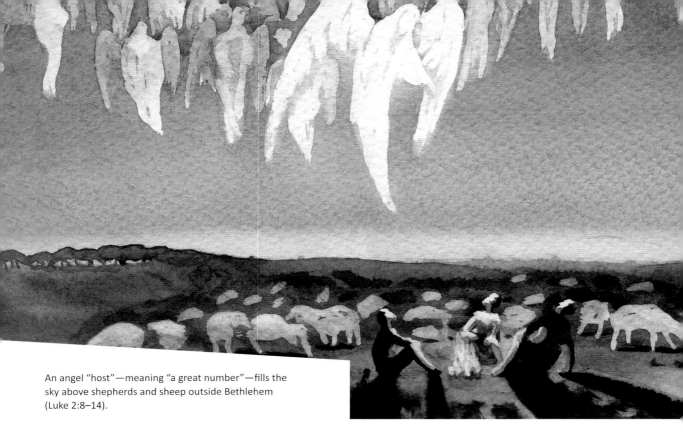

An angel "host"—meaning "a great number"—fills the sky above shepherds and sheep outside Bethlehem (Luke 2:8–14).

ANGELS, ANGELS EVERYWHERE! (LUKE 2:8–20)

Outside Bethlehem that night, some shepherds were watching over their sheep, keeping an eye out for thieves or wild animals that could drag their animals away. But the quiet of the night was broken by some amazing sounds and sights—suddenly, an angel of God appeared and the glory of God was shining all around the shepherds. They were terrified, and probably fell on their faces and trembled in fear.

But the angel quickly told the men, "Do not be afraid. See! I bring you good news of great joy which is for all people. Today, One Who saves from the punishment of sin has been born in the city of David. He is Christ the Lord. There will be something special for you to see. This is the way you will know Him. You will find the Baby with cloth around Him, lying in a place where cattle are fed" (Luke 2:10–12).

Just then, many more angels appeared on the scene, lighting up the nighttime sky, giving thanks to God, and singing, "Greatness and honor to our God in the highest heaven and peace on earth among men who please Him" (Luke 2:14).

What a scene that must have been!

After the angels returned to heaven, the shepherds looked at one another and said, "Let us go now to Bethlehem and see what has happened. The Lord has told us about this" (Luke 2:15). They hurried into town, where they found

Mary and Joseph, with the baby Jesus lying in a manger, just as the angel had said. Soon, the shepherds were telling people what they had seen and heard that night—and everyone who heard them was amazed and excited. The shepherds then returned to their flock of sheep, praising God all the way back for sending the Messiah they knew God had promised.

What an incredible night it was when Jesus was born! But that was just the beginning of the life of a man who would truly change the world.

Next, let's discuss something the Bible doesn't say very much about: Jesus growing up in Nazareth. You might be wondering why one famous part of the Christmas story didn't show up in this chapter. You'll find out as you read the next chapter!

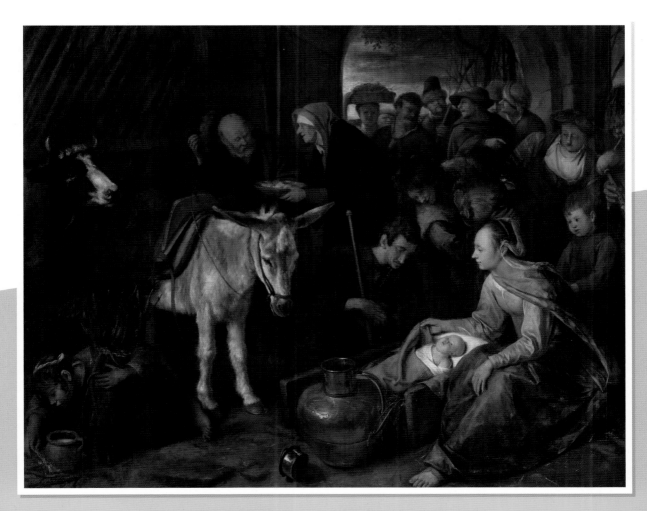

Shepherds crowd the stable where Mary cares for the newborn Jesus.

CHAPTER 4

JESUS' CHILDHOOD: WHAT WE KNOW AND WHAT WE CAN GUESS

IN THIS CHAPTER:

- Jesus dedicated at the temple in Jerusalem
- Wise men seek—and find—Jesus in Bethlehem
- Jesus' family flees to Egypt, then moves to Nazareth
- Jesus amazes people at the Jerusalem temple
- Life for a Jewish boy in first-century Galilee

Most people know about Jesus' birth—after all, we celebrate it every year at Christmastime! Many people are familiar with things Jesus did during His ministry here on earth. And most know about His death on a wooden cross, and how God the Father raised Him from the dead. But what about the things that happened in Jesus' life in between His birth and the beginning of His ministry?

The Bible doesn't tell us a lot about Jesus' childhood years, and it says nothing about Him between the ages of twelve and about thirty. But a few passages give us a quick glimpse of Jesus' boyhood. We can also figure out some things about Jesus' early years by reading clues in the Bible and by looking at Jewish history—especially at the way Jewish children were raised and taught in Israel.

Why is knowing about Jesus' childhood important? Because it reminds us that while Jesus was "God in the flesh," He was also a human being who grew from childhood to adulthood—just like any other person.

So let's start this chapter by reviewing what we know for sure—in other words, the things the Bible says about Jesus as baby and as a boy growing up in Nazareth.

Nazareth today is much larger then it was in Jesus' time. But He would have seen the same sky and hills when He looked out of His home.

DEDICATED AT THE TEMPLE (LUKE 2:21–40)

One reason Mary and Joseph were chosen to be Jesus' parents here on earth is that they both loved and obeyed God. Because they followed His instructions, they did everything required for their newborn son in the law that God had given Moses centuries before.

Jesus, Mary, and Joseph were Jewish people, and they obeyed the laws in what we now call the Old Testament. So when Jesus was eight days old, they "did the religious act of becoming a Jew on the Child" (Luke 2:21) and named Him "Jesus," just as the angel Gabriel had instructed them. That religious act is what the Bible calls "circumcision," and it was required of all Jewish males. (Remember, in Chapter 3 of this book, you read about the priest Zacharias and his

wife, Elizabeth, holding the same ceremony for John.) This circumcision probably took place in Bethlehem, at a local Jewish place of worship called a synagogue.

But there was another step God wanted Mary and Joseph to take with their son.

Have you ever been to a church service where new parents bring their babies in front of the people and promise to teach them about how to live the way God wants them to? That's often called a "baby dedication service," and the Jewish people did something similar. At the time of Jesus' birth—and for thousands of years before that—God asked the Jewish people to bring their children to the temple in Jerusalem to "dedicate" them to His service.

Faithful old Simeon and Anna, who had waited many years for God's Messiah, finally get to see Him when Mary and Joseph bring baby Jesus to the temple.

When Jesus was forty days old, Mary and Joseph traveled from Bethlehem to Jerusalem for His dedication. (By the way, Jewish baby girls were also dedicated, but that was done when they were eighty days old, not forty.) The ceremony required parents to bring a lamb as a sacrifice to the Lord, but if the family didn't have enough money for a lamb, they could bring two pigeons or turtledoves. The Bible says that Mary and Joseph brought two turtledoves, which tells us they didn't have a lot of money.

In the temple to dedicate Jesus, Mary and Joseph met an amazing man named Simeon. He lived his life to please God. He had God's Spirit on him.

Simeon wanted more than anything to see the Messiah before he died, and God had promised Simeon that he would. We don't know how long Simeon waited, but it seems like he was an old man by the time Jesus was born. Simeon continued to believe God's promise, and one day it came true!

The Bible says that the Holy Spirit led Simeon to go to the temple on the same day Jesus was dedicated. He probably didn't know why God wanted him to go that day, but he did what he was told. When Simeon saw Mary and Joseph walking into the temple holding the baby Jesus, he instantly knew who he was seeing. God's Spirit told Simeon that the little one in Mary's arms was the Savior he had been waiting to see.

Simeon approached the young family with excitement and took Jesus into his arms. He probably had tears of joy streaming down his face when he said:

"Lord, now let me die in peace, as You have said. My eyes have seen the One Who will save men from the punishment of their sins. You have made Him ready in the sight of all nations. He will be a light to shine on the people who are not Jews. He will be the shining-greatness of Your people the Jews."
LUKE 2:29–32

God had already told Mary and Joseph who Jesus really was, but they were still amazed when they heard Simeon's praise to God. Simeon also talked to Mary and Joseph about Jesus' future and how people would respond to Him.

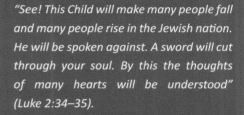

WHO SAID THAT?

"See! This Child will make many people fall and many people rise in the Jewish nation. He will be spoken against. A sword will cut through your soul. By this the thoughts of many hearts will be understood" (Luke 2:34–35).

Simeon, a man who loved God and lived for Him, spoke these words about Jesus when Mary and Joseph brought Him to the temple in Jerusalem for His dedication. Simeon's words meant that many people would believe in Jesus while many others would not. Some people would say wrong things about Him.

As Mary and Joseph listened to Simeon in the temple, an elderly woman approached them. Her name was Anna, and she was very, very old.

Anna, a prophetess, thanked God for Mary's baby, then "told the people in Jerusalem about Jesus" (Luke 2:38).

Anna was a widow whose husband had died many years before. She actually stayed day and night in the temple, where she worshiped God every day. The Bible said she was a prophet (someone who tells people what God wanted them to hear), and it also says she knew who Jesus was right away. The moment she saw Jesus, she began thanking God for sending the long-awaited Savior.

Once Mary and Joseph dedicated Jesus as God required, they left Simeon and Anna in the temple and left Jerusalem. (Just imagine how happy those old believers must have been as they watched the younger couple leave with their baby. They had seen the Savior!)

Luke's Gospel says that Jesus' family traveled back to their home in Nazareth, but many people believe they first returned to Bethlehem and stayed there for a while. Why is that important? Keep reading. . .

The traditional image of the wise men—three kings, riding camels, following a star.

SOME WISE MEN VISIT JESUS (MATTHEW 2:1–12)

Nearly every Nativity scene on display at Christmastime includes the newborn Jesus, Mary and Joseph, shepherds, and three wise men from the east who came to worship Him. (And, every year, people sing the old Christmas song, "We Three Kings.")

But the Bible doesn't specifically say that the wise men (also called "magi") visited Jesus in Bethlehem at the same time as the shepherds. It also never says there were *three* of them!

Remember, the four Gospel writers included different details in their books. Some wrote down facts the others left out, and that can make it hard to put the story of Jesus' birth and childhood in perfect order. Even Bible experts don't agree on everything. But in the following paragraphs, we'll offer a good timeline for the wise men's arrival.

There's a lot we don't know about the wise men who visited Jesus. Even though some people believe their names were Gaspar, Melchior, and Balthasar, those names come from old Christian traditions. The Bible does not name them. And the Bible never says how many wise men there were. The only number mentioned in their story is three, and that is the number of gifts they brought with them: gold, frankincense, and myrrh. (Frankincense and myrrh are pleasant-smelling substances from trees in the wise men's homeland—both were very valuable at that time). It's possible there were three wise men, but there could have been two, or many more. In those days, people traveled long distances in large groups to be safer from robbers or wild animals, so it's likely the wise men traveled in a crowd.

They may not look like much to us, but the wise men's gifts—gold, frankincense, and myrrh—were valuable and useful to Mary, Joseph, and Jesus.

WHAT DOES THIS MEAN TO ME?

"The early preacher wrote, 'You, Bethlehem of Judah, are not the least of the leaders of Judah. Out of you will come a King Who will lead My people the Jews' " (Matthew 2:5–6).

The apostle Matthew wrote these words to help his Jewish readers understand that when Jesus was born in Bethlehem, He fulfilled an Old Testament prophecy about the Messiah. Matthew was quoting directly from Micah 5:2–4.

But here's what we know for sure: the wise men were from what the Bible calls eastern lands—probably a place called Persia, which is today the country of Iran. If they were from Persia, then they would have traveled more than *eight hundred miles* to see Jesus. They were very smart men who studied the stars and planets, and they had probably read old writings telling them that a new star would appear when a great king was born. Some believe that they had read some of the Old Testament prophecies about the coming Messiah.

The wise men found their way from their homeland to Judea—where Bethlehem and Jerusalem were located—by following what they called "his star." Many Christians now call it "the star of Bethlehem" or "the Christmas star." Some people believe this unusual light in the sky was a comet, and others think it was a supernova—a faraway, exploding star—that appeared in the night sky around that time. Still others say it wasn't a natural object at all, but something God had miraculously placed in the sky so the wise men could follow it to find Jesus. Whatever

it was, the wise men from the east knew it was a sign from God. The sign said that the King of the Jews had been born.

Now, about the timing of the wise men's visit to Jesus.

It's likely that the wise men first arrived in Jerusalem some time after Jesus' dedication at the temple. The Bible says that after Anna saw Jesus, she began telling people in Jerusalem

Even if the Christmas star was a "natural" comet, it was still a miracle—because it appeared just at the time and place to lead the wise men to young Jesus.

about Him. Word of Jesus' birth probably spread quickly throughout the city because the Jewish people there "were looking for the One to save them from the punishment of their sins and to set them free" (Luke 2:38).

When the wise men arrived in Jerusalem, they asked, "Where is the King of the Jews Who has been born? We have seen His star in the East. We have come to worship Him" (Matthew 2:2). That probably added to the excitement among the Jewish people, and it wasn't long before word got back to King Herod that the wise men had been asking about Jesus. This worried Herod because he didn't want another king competing for the people's loyalty.

"Herod the Great" was the Roman king of Judea, who became king around 37 BC and held that office until his death, which was between 4 and 1 BC. (As we noted earlier, most historians and Bible experts agree that Jesus wasn't born in the year zero, but instead was born between 6 and 4 BC.) Herod was a very bad man who treated many people in Judea cruelly. He didn't like anyone to challenge his authority in any way, and he killed many people who tried to stand up to him. Herod often did things to disrespect the Jewish religion. Even though he reconstructed their temple, he didn't do it to honor God—he just wanted Judea's capital to reflect well on himself.

When he heard about Jesus' birth, Herod hatched a plan—a *really evil* plan. He met with the Jewish religious leaders in Jerusalem and asked them where their Messiah was to be born. They told Herod that the scriptures said He would born in Bethlehem, a small town about six miles south of Jerusalem. Herod called the magi to meet with him and told them they could find the King of the Jews in Bethlehem. He also asked them to come back to him after they had visited the Messiah and tell him where He was—so that he could go and worship Him too. But Herod didn't plan on worshiping Jesus at all. He wanted to *kill* the new King before He had a chance to take Herod's place in Judea.

The wise men left Herod and continued to follow the light in the sky to Bethlehem. By the time the wise men arrived, Jesus and His parents had moved into a house, and the light stopped over the house where they were. The wise men's first response to seeing Jesus was to bow down and worship Him. Then they gave Him their gifts.

The Bible doesn't say how long the wise men stayed in Bethlehem, but it tells us that they never returned to speak to Herod about Jesus. They took another way home because God had warned them in a dream not to return to Jerusalem.

King Herod asks the wise men to tell him when they find Jesus, so "I can go and worship Him also" (Matthew 2:8). He really wanted to kill Jesus.

TO EGYPT AND BACK (MATTHEW 2:13–23)

After the wise men left Bethlehem to return to their homeland, Joseph was visited by an angel in the night. "Get up!" the angel told him. "Flee to Egypt with the child and his mother. Stay there until I tell you to return, because Herod is going to search for the child to kill him" (Matthew 2:13 NLT).

Joseph didn't even wait until morning to get his family moving toward Egypt. He got up out of bed that very night, got Jesus and Mary ready to travel, and headed for Egypt. God knew what Herod was planning to do, and He wasn't going to let an evil king stand in the way of His plans.

When Herod realized that the wise men had ignored his order for them to tell him where Jesus was, he became so angry that he commanded his soldiers to kill all boys two years old or younger in and around Bethlehem. Because of the wise men, Herod knew the place and time of Jesus' birth. By this point, though, Jesus, Mary, and Joseph had already left for Egypt.

Jesus stayed in Egypt with His parents until after Herod the Great died. Jesus may have been about two years old at the time. When it was safe for Jesus' family to return to Judea, an angel of God appeared to Joseph in another dream. "Get up," the angel said. "Take the young Child and His mother and go into the land of the Jews. Those who tried to kill the young Child are dead" (Matthew 2:20).

Joseph again did exactly as the angel told him. He took Jesus and Mary and headed back toward the land of Israel. But when Joseph heard that Herod's son Archelaus was the new ruler there, he was afraid to go to Judea. So instead, he and his young family traveled to Galilee and settled in Nazareth, Mary and Joseph's original hometown.

ONE AMAZING BOY! (LUKE 2:41–52)

After the journey to Egypt, there is only one other scene of Jesus' childhood in the Gospels.

IT'S IN THE BIBLE!

During the night he got up and left with the young Child and His mother for Egypt. He stayed there until Herod died. This happened as the Lord had said through an early preacher, "I called My Son out of Egypt." (Matthew 2:14–15).

Jesus lived in Nazareth until He started His "earthly ministry" when He was about thirty years old. He probably grew up like most Jewish boys in that part of the world. The Bible says Jesus was a healthy boy who grew up to become bigger and stronger every day. He probably helped Joseph in his work as a carpenter, and He probably studied the Bible in school, like the other Jewish boys living in Israel.

The famous pyramids of Egypt. Mary, Joseph, and young Jesus had to escape into Egypt to avoid King Herod's murderous plan.

Young Jesus was "filled with wisdom, and the loving-favor of God was on Him" (Luke 2:40). All Jewish boys at that time studied the Bible in school and learned about God's rules for life and His promises. So Jesus probably started attending school when He was around five years old. A collection of traditional Jewish writings called the Mishnah tells us how young boys were educated at that time. The schools were like the ones kids go to today in one way: students learned the simplest and most basic things first before moving on to more difficult and complicated topics.

Schools were connected with the local synagogues, and each community would hire its own teacher, called a "rabbi." The children started learning to read scripture (what we know as the Old Testament) at four or five years of age. At ten, they learned the Mishnah, and at twelve or thirteen, they were responsible for keeping God's commandments.

In addition to school, Jesus probably learned about the Bible at home too. Mary and Joseph built their life on what the Bible taught about God's love, His rules for life, and the promises He had made to them about Jesus. You can imagine that the family talked a lot about the scriptures and that they prayed to God together.

Most children who grow up in a home like Joseph and Mary's learn a lot about God's love and how He wants them to live. But Jesus understood the Bible and all rules and promises a lot better than other schoolchildren, even the ones who lived in good homes like His. There was something very special about this boy!

When Jesus was twelve years old, He put His learning and wisdom on display—and amazed some older, wiser men in the process.

As a boy, Jesus probably learned to read on a scroll of scripture something like this.

In those days, Jewish people from around the world would travel to Jerusalem once a year to take part in a Jewish celebration called "Passover." Mary and Joseph were no different, making the trip from Nazareth to remember God's love and protection of His people during their escape from slavery in Egypt. At twelve, Jesus was of the age when Jewish children celebrated Passover with the grown-ups. So the family packed everything they'd need for a seventy-mile trip and joined a large group of people to head to Jerusalem.

Mary and Joseph and Jesus stayed eight days in Jerusalem, and then it was time to head home to Nazareth. So Mary and Joseph packed up their belongings and joined the big caravan heading north.

Though Jesus' parents had left Jerusalem, He stayed behind. At first, Mary and Joseph didn't even realize He wasn't with the crowd heading back to Galilee. They probably assumed He was with friends or more distant family members. But when Mary and Joseph realized that Jesus wasn't in the larger group, they felt the panic any parent would in that situation. They started looking for Jesus and asking their friends and relatives if they knew where He was. But nobody knew!

Imagine how Mary and Joseph must have felt when they realized that the son God had so miraculously given them was missing. They left their traveling group and hurried back to Jerusalem to look for their missing son.

Finally, after three full days, Mary and Joseph found Jesus. He hadn't been playing with other kids in the area, and He hadn't gotten Himself lost when the people from Nazareth started for home. Instead, He was sitting near the temple, talking with some Jewish religious teachers, asking these learned men questions and answering their questions.

These teachers were well educated men. They knew and understood the Bible, and they knew how to teach others what they knew. But they had never seen a boy like Jesus. The men were amazed that a boy so young could understand the Word of God the way He did. The Bible doesn't say whether the teachers realized that Jesus was the Messiah, but one thing they did know: this was no ordinary kid!

Joseph and Mary must have been relieved to find Jesus safe. But at the same time, they didn't know quite what to make of what they

were seeing. They might have expected their twelve-year-old son to go to the temple and ask someone to keep Him safe and give Him something to eat while He waited for His parents to come find Him. Yet there Jesus was, sitting with some of the smartest people in Jerusalem, calmly talking with them.

Mary was the first to speak. "Son," she said, probably with tears in her eyes, "why have you done this to us? Your father and I have been frantic, searching for you everywhere" (Luke 2:48 NLT).

But Jesus simply answered, "Why did you need to search? Didn't you know that I must be in my Father's house?" (Luke 2:49 NLT).

Mary didn't understand what Jesus meant when He said that, but from that day on, she remembered what had happened and Jesus' words to her. Jesus, though, understood

WHAT DOES THIS MEAN TO ME?

PASSOVER

Joseph and Mary went to Jerusalem every year to celebrate the Passover. The Passover started when the Israelites put lamb's blood around their doorposts and the Lord "passed over" their homes in the final plague on Egypt. All the firstborn in Egypt died because Pharaoh refused to let the Israelites return to their homeland of Canaan. God told the people to remember the Passover every year after they finally left Egypt (see Exodus 12:12–14).

everything about the situation. Even at age twelve—and probably well before that—He knew who He was. Jesus realized that He wasn't like the other kids at school. He knew that God had sent Him to earth, and He knew what His Father in heaven had sent Him to do. Jesus knew that He was the Son of God!

Twelve-year-old Jesus discusses God's law with the religious teachers in Jerusalem. This story is the only information we have of Jesus' life from the time of the wise men's visit until He began preaching and teaching around age thirty.

Mary and Joseph find twelve-year-old Jesus in the temple at Jerusalem. ""Why were you looking for Me?" He asked. "Do you not know that I must be in My Father's house?" (Luke 2:49)

After the visit to the temple, Jesus and His parents returned to Nazareth. The Bible says that Jesus grew in wisdom, in physical maturity, and in the favor of God and all the people who knew Him.

Jesus spent the next eighteen years of His life growing and preparing Himself for the tremendous work His Father in heaven had called Him to do. He probably worked with his earthly father, Joseph, as a carpenter. People who knew Jesus as a young man in Nazareth called Him "just a carpenter" in Mark 6:3 (NLT).

As He was growing up in Nazareth, the Bible says Jesus obeyed His parents (Luke 2:51). That makes sense, because the Bible indicates Jesus perfectly kept the laws from the Old Testament— including God's commandment that children honor their mother and father. You can read that commandment in Exodus 20:12.

Many kids have brothers and sisters, and Jesus was no different. He shared His home with boys named James, Joseph, Judas, and Simon. He also had some sisters, but the Bible doesn't tell us how many or what their names were (Mark 6:3).

Everything Jesus learned as a child, everything He did, and everything He experienced as a son of Mary and Joseph and a brother to His siblings—all of that helped make Him ready for the life ahead of Him. When the time was right, Jesus began a traveling ministry that would change the world, starting with the land of Israel.

You can read about that ministry—and maybe learn a new thing or two about Jesus—in the next few chapters of this book!

WHAT DOES THIS MEAN?

You know how Jesus is often called "Jesus Christ"? The word *Christ* is not actually part of Jesus' name, but a title for who He is. It comes from the Greek word *Christos*, and it means "the anointed"—someone God had chosen. When used in the Bible, *Christ* is the Greek translation for the Hebrew word *Messiah*.

A man in Nazareth, Jesus' hometown, demonstrates carpentry as it probably looked in Jesus' time.

CHAPTER 5

FOLLOWING JESUS' FOOTSTEPS ON EARTH

IN THIS CHAPTER:

- Jesus' baptism in the Jordan River
- Jesus tempted in the wilderness
- Jesus calls twelve men to follow Him
- The travels of Jesus and His disciples
- What Jesus said about who He was
- Some amazing miracles

Think about the stories you've read or heard of Jesus' life on earth. Which ones come to mind first? The time He fed five thousand people with a few loaves of bread and some dried fish? Or the time He brought a dead man named Lazarus back to life? Or the time He walked on the water in front of His stunned followers?

Isn't it amazing to think that the Son of God—the man the Bible says was God in human form—actually lived here on earth and did all the incredible things the Bible describes?

The Gospel of Luke says that Jesus started His "earthly ministry" when He "was about thirty years old" (Luke 3:23). Between that time and the day Jesus died on a cross, He called twelve men to be His closest followers, and then walked countless miles with them, preaching the greatest sermons ever heard, healing huge numbers of really sick people, bringing some people back to life, and feeding thousands with just a little bit of food. He also turned water into wine, calmed storms with His voice, and walked on water. And while He was doing all that, Jesus set the greatest example ever of the life God wants all of us to live.

This story started when He met with a very special man God had sent to prepare people to meet Jesus.

John the Baptist pours water over Jesus in this painting from an Austrian church. Many artists show Jesus being baptized in this way, though some churches believe He was dunked into the water (or "immersed") because Matthew 3:16 says the heavens were opened and the Holy Spirit appeared like a dove "when Jesus came up out of the water."

JOHN BAPTIZES JESUS (MATTHEW 3:13–17)

Remember back in Chapter 3 of this book, when you read about the births of both Jesus and John the Baptist? Jesus and John were related through their mothers, and it's not hard to think that they got to know one another pretty well when they were kids—even though they did not grow up in the same town.

As Jesus was about to start His ministry on earth, John was busy telling others that they needed to ask God to forgive them for the wrong things they had done. John spoke about "repentance," and living lives that pleased God. John knew he wasn't the promised Messiah. He had been sent by God to prepare people to see Jesus.

Just as Jesus would fulfill many Old Testament promises of the coming Savior, John fulfilled God's promise of a messenger who would lead the way. The Gospel of Mark put it this like this:

This is the Good News about Jesus the Messiah, the Son of God. It began just as the prophet Isaiah had written: "Look, I am sending my messenger ahead of you, and he will prepare your way. He is a voice shouting in the wilderness, 'Prepare the way for the LORD's coming! Clear the road for him!' "
MARK 1:1–3 NLT

John the Baptist wasn't anything you might expect a preacher to be. He wore clothes made of scratchy camel hair, and he had a leather belt. He didn't have a house, but instead traveled all around looking for people to preach to. He probably slept outside most of the time, unless some nice people offered to let him spend the night in their home. Weirdest of all, John lived on a diet of honey and locusts (kind of like a grasshopper).

Does that look like lunch to you? It was for John the Baptist!

John probably didn't have much to call his own. He lived a simple life, not really caring about things. To John, it was much more important to do what God wanted him to do. He loved telling people about the good things God could do in their lives, and he wanted to get people ready to meet Jesus.

Some people thought John might be the Messiah they had been waiting for. But John told them that he wasn't—he was preaching to prepare the world for the real Messiah, the Savior. When religious leaders from Jerusalem learned many people were going out to hear John preach, they traveled to Bethany (about two miles away) to question him. They wanted to know who he was and why he thought he should be preaching to people and baptizing them.

John answered, "I baptize with water. But there is One standing among you Whom you do not know. He is the One Who is coming after me. I am not good enough to get down and help Him take off His shoes" (John 1:26–27). John also explained that while he baptized people with water, Jesus would baptize with the Holy Spirit (Matthew 3:11).

The very next day, Jesus approached John near the Jordan River, asking to be baptized.

When Jesus waded into the water, John didn't want to baptize Him. John didn't feel worthy, and he told Jesus that it should be the other way around—Jesus should baptize John! But Jesus insisted, assuring John that it was God's will.

So John baptized his relative and Savior. When Jesus came up out of the water, the Holy Spirit came down on Him, and He heard God's voice saying, "This is my much-loved Son. I am very happy with Him" (Matthew 3:17).

After He was baptized, Jesus spent forty days in the wilderness, where He was with wild animals but angels took care of Him." (Mark 1:13).

WHEN JESUS SAID "NO!" TO THE DEVIL (MATTHEW 4:1–11, MARK 1:12–13, LUKE 4:1–13)

Can you remember the last time you were tempted to do something you knew was wrong? Everyone is tempted to do the wrong thing sometimes. Even Jesus was tempted here on earth! The Bible tells us that the devil appeared to Jesus personally, tempting Him to do things He knew weren't part of God's plan. But the temptation itself *was* part of His Father's plan.

After His baptism, Jesus went out to the desert to pray. He didn't just pray though, He also fasted, meaning He didn't eat anything at all—for forty days! In both the Old Testament and the New Testament alike, people who loved God often fasted when they prayed. When they did that, it showed their commitment to focus only on God. They were showing how serious they were about seeking Him and praying to Him. Jesus did the same thing. Since He was about to begin three years of traveling, teaching, performing miracles, and sacrificing Himself for our sins, He knew He needed to stay focused on His Father's plan.

The devil knew what God had in mind, and he tried his best to distract Jesus. During Jesus' forty days of fasting and praying, the devil thought he had the Lord right where he wanted Him. Knowing Jesus was hungry from not eating for so long, the devil approached Him and said, "If You are the Son of God, tell these stones to be made into bread" (Matthew 4:3).

Jesus could have done that easily—He had created the whole universe in the beginning. But Jesus knew that God the Father had taken Him into the desert so they could talk with one another. He wasn't about to let the devil keep Him from that important time with His Father in heaven, so He said, "No! The Scriptures say, 'People do not live by bread alone, but by every word that comes from the mouth of God' " (Matthew 4:4 NLT).

The devil then took Jesus to the highest part of the temple in Jerusalem and said to Him, "If you are the Son of God, jump off! For the Scriptures say, 'He will order his angels to protect you. And they will hold you up with their hands so you won't even hurt your foot on a stone' " (Matthew 4:6 NLT). But Jesus responded, "The Scriptures also say, 'You must not test the LORD your God' " (Matthew 4:7 NLT).

WHAT DOES THIS MEAN TO ME?

We have a great Religious Leader Who has made the way for man to go to God. He is Jesus, the Son of God, Who has gone to heaven to be with God. Let us keep our trust in Jesus Christ. Our Religious Leader understands how weak we are. Christ was tempted in every way we are tempted, but He did not sin (Hebrews 4:14–15).

Jesus was the Son of God, but He was also a human being who could be tempted to do the wrong things. These verses tell us that Jesus understands that we are weak when we are tempted to sin. But He also promises to give us strength to say "no" to temptation.

But the devil wasn't about to give up. He took Jesus to the top of a mountain and showed Him all the kingdoms of the world. Then Satan said, "I will give it all to you if you will kneel down and worship me" (Matthew 4:9 NLT). Now Jesus was finished with the devil for the day. "Get out of here, Satan," He said. "For the Scriptures say, 'You must worship the Lord your God and serve him only' " (Matthew 4:10 NLT).

When Jesus was tempted, all three times He answered the devil by quoting the Bible. When He did that, He showed two important things: (1) His commitment to do what His Father in heaven had sent Him to do, and (2) the power the words in the Bible have to help *us* fight off temptation.

Now it was time for Jesus to get busy! The Gospel of Matthew says that from the time of His baptism on, Jesus began preaching this message: "Be sorry for your sins and turn from them. The holy nation of heaven is near" (Matthew 4:17).

Satan tried—and failed—three times to get Jesus to do something wrong. To defeat the temptations, Jesus quoted God's Word, something we can do too.

The first four disciples Jesus chose were fishermen on the Sea of Galilee. They were also business partners and two sets of brothers: Peter and Andrew, and James and John.

TWELVE OF JESUS' CLOSEST FRIENDS (MATTHEW 4:18–22, MARK 1:16–34, LUKE 5:1–11)

Right after Jesus fought off the devil's temptations, He began calling a group of twelve men who would travel around with Him for the next three years. These men are called sometimes Jesus' disciples, but they are also called His "apostles."

These guys weren't the smartest or most talented people Jesus could have chosen. In fact, they all had flaws. But Jesus hand-picked them, and then He spent a lot of time teaching them how to live. He prepared them to spread the message of salvation around the world after He returned to heaven.

Here's a list of Jesus' disciples and some things we know about them:

- **Peter and Andrew:** These men were brothers, fishermen by trade, and they were the first disciples Jesus called. They lived in a place called Capernaum, a fishing village on the northern coast of the Sea of Galilee. The Gospel of Mark says, "Jesus said to them, 'Follow Me. I will make you fish for men!' At once they left their nets and followed Him" (Mark 1:17–18). If you want to read more about Jesus calling Peter and Andrew, look at Luke 5:1–11.

- **James and John:** They were the second pair of brothers Jesus invited to follow Him. Like Peter and Andrew, they were fishermen from Capernaum. Jesus called the pair "sons of thunder" (Mark 10:35–45), perhaps because they spoke without thinking. Jesus called James and John while they were in their boat working on their nets; they immediately left their father, Zebedee, to continue the work without them.

- **Philip:** A day after calling James and John, Jesus invited Philip to follow Him. Philip was from Bethsaida, another coastal village near the Sea of Galilee. After meeting Jesus, Philip brought the next disciple in this list to meet Him too.

- **Bartholomew:** The four Gospels don't tell us much about Bartholomew, other than that he was one of Jesus' twelve apostles. It's believed that he was also called Nathanael (see John 1:45–51). When Bartholomew/Nathanael first met Jesus, the Lord said, "Now here is a genuine son of Israel—a man of complete integrity" (John 1:47 NLT). That's high praise, coming from the Son of God!

- **Matthew:** He was an unlikely candidate to be one of Jesus' twelve disciples. Matthew, also called Levi, was a tax collector—and Jewish people didn't take kindly to his type. In fact, they *hated* tax-collectors. Matthew was working at his collection booth when Jesus called him (Mark 2:13–17). How important was Matthew? Well, if you've read the Gospel of Matthew, you've read something this disciple wrote!

- **Thomas:** Ever hear of someone called a "doubting Thomas"? That phrase started with this apostle, who needed proof that he was really seeing Jesus after the resurrection (see John 20:24–29). His nickname, Didymus, means "twin."

- **James:** Several men named James are listed in the New Testament, and two of them were disciples of Jesus. This one—not the brother of John—is identified as the son of a man named Alphaeus. He has been called "James the Less." Very little else is known about him.

- **Simon:** This disciple is mentioned only four times in the Bible—in the Gospels of Matthew, Mark, and Luke, and in the book of Acts (1:13).

- **Thaddeus:** The Bible doesn't tell us much about Thaddeus, but indicates he may also have been known by the name Jude or Judas. Some Bible experts believe he wrote the epistle of Jude, but most think the half-brother of Jesus did.

- **Judas Iscariot:** Judas is identified as the disciple who betrayed Jesus. When He chose His disciples, Jesus knew the future of each one—so why would He pick a man He knew would turn against Him? Because Judas's betrayal was part of God's plan to bring salvation to the world.

HITTING THE ROAD

The apostle John—not John the Baptist—wrote in his Gospel that Jesus "became human flesh and lived among us. We saw His shining-greatness. This greatness is given only to a much-loved Son from His Father. He was full of loving-favor and truth" (John 1:14).

John's words hint at Jesus' glory ("shining-greatness") as God. But most of the four Gospels describe Jesus' earthly ministry. These books show that during the last three years of His life on earth, Jesus traveled around Israel with His disciples. He stopped in many places to teach people how to love God, doing miracles that showed He really was the Son of God.

All of Jesus' earthly ministry took place in the land of Israel, which was under control of the Roman Empire. In the four Gospels, you can read about the places Jesus visited and things He did and said in each of them. Here are details on a few of those places:

- **Galilee**: Jesus spent a lot of His time in the region called Galilee, especially in the town of Capernaum, home of the apostles Peter and Andrew. Galilee is in the northern area of Israel, bordering on the Sea of Galilee, which plays a big part in Jesus' story. Jesus' boyhood hometown of Nazareth was in Galilee, and He visited other Galilean villages including Cana, Nain, Bethsaida, and Chorazin.
- **Jerusalem**: The Gospels include several stories of Jesus visiting the city of Jerusalem, which was in the Roman province of Judea. There are two examples of Jesus entering the

temple in Jerusalem and angrily driving out merchants, people who were making money off the worshipers. Later in this book, you'll read about Jesus' final days on earth, which He spent mostly in Jerusalem.

Jesus surprises His disciples by speaking to a Samaritan woman at the well of Sychar.

- **Samaria**: During Jesus' time, Jewish people tried hard to avoid traveling through Samaria, an area between Judea to the south and Galilee to the north. Jews looked down on Samaritans, viewing them as impure since their family lines included other nationalities. But Jesus didn't see people that way, so He was happy to travel through Samaria. While there, He met and talked with a Samaritan woman, telling her many truths about Himself. (You can read the whole story in John 4:4–26.)

- **Bethany**: Three of Jesus' closest friends—sisters Mary and Martha and their brother Lazarus—lived in a small town called Bethany. It was located just a few miles east of Jerusalem. In Bethany, Jesus raised Lazarus from the dead. In the week leading up to His arrest, trial, and crucifixion, He spent His nights in Bethany. One evening that week, Jesus and the apostles had dinner in the house of a man named Simon. At dinner, Jesus' friend Mary washed His feet with perfume and dried them with her hair.

- **The Desert**: The Gospel of Luke says that Jesus "was led by the Holy Spirit to a desert" (4:1). He stayed there forty days to fast and pray. During that time, the

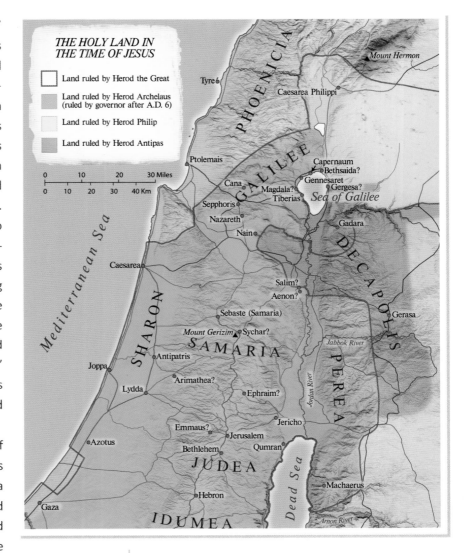

THE HOLY LAND IN THE TIME OF JESUS

- Land ruled by Herod the Great
- Land ruled by Herod Archelaus (ruled by governor after A.D. 6)
- Land ruled by Herod Philip
- Land ruled by Herod Antipas

devil tried unsuccessfully to get Jesus to sin. This desert was in Judea, probably an unpopulated area east of the Jordan River.

- **The Mount of Transfiguration**: People aren't exactly sure which mountain was the "Mount of Transfiguration." But we know that Jesus took three of His apostles—Peter, James, and John—to the top of a mountain, where they saw Moses and the prophet Elijah talking with Jesus. They also saw Jesus' "shining-greatness"

and heard a voice from heaven saying, "This is My Son, the One I have chosen. Listen to Him!" (You can read this story in Luke 9:28–36.)

This book doesn't include every place Jesus traveled or everything He did and said. To get the full story, you'll need to read through Matthew, Mark, Luke, and John. For now, let's consider some very important things Jesus said about Himself.

CHAPTER 6

WHAT JESUS SAID—AND WHAT IT MEANS

IN THIS CHAPTER:

- Jesus' teaching in the Sermon on the Mount
- Jesus' teaching through stories called parables
- Jesus talks with a religious leader about being "born again"

Have you ever heard someone use phrases like "an eye for an eye, a tooth for a tooth" or "the blind leading the blind"? How about "wolves in sheep's clothing" or "he who lives by the sword, dies by the sword"?

These are just a few examples of things Jesus said that people still say today—even when they're not talking about Jesus or the Bible. But He had a lot more to say than just memorable phrases. A lot of what Jesus said truly changed the world.

Jesus spent a lot of time teaching. He shared very important stuff about who He was, who God the Father is, and how His followers should live, think, and treat other people. Sometimes Jesus taught just one person, and sometimes He taught small groups. On other occasions, He taught large crowds.

What were some of the important truths Jesus taught? For one thing, that people needed to turn away from doing wrong things and confess their sin to God (Matthew 4:17). And that people should "take up [their] cross and follow Me" (Matthew 16:24). He taught that people needed to have faith in God (Mark 11:22) and that they must be "like a little child" before they could enter the kingdom of God (Matthew 18:3).

Some people eagerly listened to Jesus. They knew God had sent Him to earth—even if they didn't fully understand why. Some people loved His teaching so much that they decided to follow Him. But other people heard what Jesus had to say and just went back to their daily lives. Still others didn't like what Jesus had to say at all. Some became so angry about Jesus' words that they wanted to kill Him!

In the coming pages, you'll see some of the things Jesus taught—just the highlights, we could say. But as you read, remember that you won't find everything Jesus said or taught—you'll need to go to your Bible for that.

Let's start with Jesus' teaching that Christians call "the Sermon on the Mount."

Many people believe Jesus' "sermon on the moun took place here, overlooking the Sea of Galilee.

THE GREATEST SERMON EVER PREACHED (MATTHEW 5–7)

One time, a big crowd of people gathered on the shore of the Sea of Galilee (also known as Lake Gennesaret), near Capernaum, a small fishing town. Jesus went to the side of a hill and started teaching people in a way they'd never been taught before.

The crowd listened closely as Jesus delivered the greatest sermon anyone has ever preached. He talked about how people could live to please God, how they should treat others, and how they could think good thoughts.

HOW TO BE HAPPY

Jesus started His sermon by giving the people a list of blessings now called "Beatitudes." (That's a word from the old Latin language that means "happy," "blessed," or "fortunate.") There are nine Beatitudes listed in Matthew's Gospel. Most Bible experts believe the first eight were for the crowds gathered at the hillside that day, while the ninth was for those who had been following Jesus.

Here is how Jesus described blessed (or happy) people:

- "Those who know there is nothing good in themselves are happy, because the holy nation of heaven is theirs" (Matthew 5:3).
- "Those who have sorrow are happy, because they will be comforted." (Matthew 5:4).

- "Those who have no pride in their hearts are happy, because the earth will be given to them" (Matthew 5:5).
- "Those who are hungry and thirsty to be right with God are happy, because they will be filled" (Matthew 5:6).
- "Those who show loving-kindness are happy, because they will have loving-kindness shown to them" (Matthew 5:7).
- "Those who have a pure heart are happy, because they will see God" (Matthew 5:8).
- "Those who make peace are happy, because they will be called the sons of God" (Matthew 5:9).
- "Those who have it very hard for doing right are happy, because the holy nation of heaven is theirs" (Matthew 5:10).

Those are the first eight Beatitudes, that Jesus shared with the large crowd. The ninth, which was probably just for the disciples, was this: "You are happy when people act and talk in a bad way to you and make it very hard for you and tell bad things and lies about you because you trust in Me. Be glad and full of joy because your reward will be much in heaven. They made it very hard for the early preachers who lived a long time before you" (5:11–12).

MORE GREAT TEACHING FROM THE MOUNT

After Jesus spoke this list of things that make people happy and blessed, He shared some very simple teaching about how they should live. By living Jesus' way, people would be "salt" and "light" in the world around them (Matthew 5:13–16). Salt keeps food from spoiling, so Jesus was saying His followers would help to keep the world good. People need light to know where they're going, so Jesus was saying His followers would direct others to His truth. But Jesus went even further when He told the people that it's important to obey God from the heart—not just do the right thing because they think they have to. He taught the crowd some important truths about how the law of Moses really applied to them. Jesus said, in what we now know as Matthew 5:

- That refusing to forgive someone or talking bad about that person is as bad in God's eyes as killing that person (5:21–26).

Jesus called Himself "the light of the world" (John 8:12) and said His followers would be "the light of the world" as well (Matthew 5:14). What Jesus meant was that His teaching and Christians' example would show the world how to live.

- That looking at a woman with wrong thoughts was as bad as committing sin with her (5:27–30).
- That God expects people to honor their marriage vows, even though the culture allows them to get divorced (5:31–32).
- That you should always be honest with people and keep your word (5:33–37).

"Do not promise by heaven. It is the place where God is. Do not promise by earth. It is where He rests His feet. . . . Do not promise by your head. . . . Let your yes be YES. Let your no be NO. Anything more than this comes from the devil" (Matthew 5:34–37).

WHAT DOES THAT MEAN TO ME?

"I tell you, do not use strong words when you make a promise. Do not promise by heaven. It is the place where God is. Do not promise by earth. It is where He rests His feet. . . . Let your yes be YES. Let your no be NO. Anything more than this comes from the devil" (Matthew 5:34–35, 37).

God wants you to be a person of your word, someone who follows through with what you've said. Then people will trust you, simply because you always do what you say you'll do.

- That we should not pray or fast so that others will see it and think better of us. Instead, we should get alone with God and pray in private. Not only that, we should forgive other people so that God can hear our prayers (6:5–18).
- That above everything else, we should seek what is best for God's eternal kingdom (6:19–34).

- That you shouldn't try to get even with people when they do things to hurt or anger you (5:38–42).
- That you should love everyone, even those who don't love you in return (5:43–48).

Matthew 6 tells us that Jesus told His listeners about devotion to God and what that should look like in the life of a Christian. He told them:

- We should give generously without expecting others to reward us or say good things about us (6:1–4).

Jesus taught His followers to "knock" on God's door in prayer. "Everyone who asks receives what he asks for. Everyone who looks finds what he is looking for. Everyone who knocks has the door opened to him" (Matthew 7:8).

In Matthew 7, the final chapter that reports the Sermon on the Mount, Jesus discussed our relationships with other Christians and with God. (Yes, *God* wants us to have a personal relationship with Him!) Jesus told the crowd:

- That before we tell others that they've done wrong, we should make sure we're doing the things that please God (7:1–6).
- That we should ask God, our loving heavenly Father, for the things we need, knowing that He loves us and wants to do good things for for us (7:7–11).
- That we should treat others the way we want to be treated (7:12).
- That there is only one way to God—through Jesus Christ (7:13–14).
- That we should watch out for people who teach the wrong things (7:15–20).
- That our relationship with Jesus is based first on our faith in Him, not on the things we say or do (7:21–23)

INGREDIENTS FOR GOOD PRAYER (MATHEW 6:5–13)

Jesus knew that the people listening to Him had seen some bad examples of prayer. Sometimes the Jewish religious leaders would pray loudly, in public, to draw attention to themselves. So Jesus took time to teach the people how to pray in a way that really connected with God.

Jesus said people must be sincere when they speak to God. They should never pray just to look good to others. He urged His listeners to get alone with God, so they could pray without being distracted. And He told them that they should not just repeat the same things over and over when they prayed—they should pray from their hearts and speak to God like they would any other person. Finally, Jesus taught that people could believe that their prayers would be answered because their Father in heaven knows what they need before they even ask.

Even though Jesus was God in human flesh, He prayed often to His Father in heaven. And he taught us many important things about prayer.

Then Jesus gave the people a model for prayer, something we now call "the Lord's Prayer":

"Our Father in heaven, Your name is holy. May Your holy nation come. What You want done, may it be done on earth as it is in heaven. Give us the bread we need today. Forgive us our sins as we forgive those who sin against us. Do not let us be tempted, but keep us from sin. Your nation is holy. You have power and shining-greatness forever. Let it be so."
MATTHEW 6:9–13

A lot of people have memorized the Lord's Prayer and like to recite it word for word. There's nothing wrong with that, but Jesus didn't give this prayer just to be read back to God. It's an example of *how* people should pray. You could say it's a recipe for prayer, and here are the ingredients:

- When Jesus said, "Our Father in heaven," He meant that everyone should pray to the God who sent Him to earth, the God who identified Himself as our heavenly Father.

- When Jesus said, "Your name is holy," He meant that we are to praise God for what He really is—perfect and completely above human beings.

- When Jesus said, "May Your holy nation come. What You want done, may it be done on earth as it is in heaven," He meant that we should ask God to do what *He* wants to do, not what *we* want in our own lives and world.

- When Jesus said, "Give us the bread we need today," He meant that we should trust God to give us the things we need for life.

- When Jesus said, "Forgive us our sins as we forgive those who sin against us," He was reminding us that we should confess our sins to God—and that we should forgive others when they do things that upset us.

- And when Jesus said, "Do not let us be tempted, but keep us from sin," He wanted us to ask for God's help to overcome temptation, our desire to do and say the things that make Him unhappy.

HOW TO BE "GOLDEN"

Have you ever heard of "the Golden Rule"? Jesus didn't use that phrase, but the Golden Rule is one of His best-known teachings. It goes like this: "Do for other people whatever you would like to have them do for you. This is what the Jewish Law and the early preachers said" (Matthew 7:12).

Jesus knew He was talking to people who could be selfish and inconsiderate of others—just

like all of us today! But He also knew that God had already told people how they should treat each other. The Golden Rule just simplified all of the earlier laws, so we could remember to treat other people with kindness, fairness, patience, forgiveness, and courtesy.

Think about how you want people to treat you. Do you like it when people are nice? Jesus says to be nice to them first. Do you like it when someone offers to help you? Jesus says to help others first. Do you like it when people forgive you after you've made a mistake? Jesus says to forgive others when they mess up. Do you like it when people include you in their circle of friends? Jesus says to include others, especially when you know they've been feeling left out.

When Jesus said, "Do for other people whatever you would like to have them do for you," He didn't mean we should only be kind to people who were kind to us first. He didn't mean we should only be kind to those who already like us. In fact, earlier in the Sermon on the Mount, Jesus said:

"But I tell you, love those who hate you. Respect and give thanks for those who say bad things to you. Do good to those who hate you. Pray for those who do bad things to you and who make it hard for you. Then you may be the sons of your Father Who is in heaven. His sun shines on bad people and on good people. He sends rain on those who are right with God and on those who are not right with God. If you love those who love you, what reward can you expect from that? Do not even the tax-gatherers do that? If you say hello only to the people you like, are you doing any more than others? The people who do not know God do that much."
MATTHEW 5:44–47

The Sermon on the Mount is well worth your time to read from beginning to end. But that's not Jesus' only great teaching. Let's look next at the way He taught using stories.

Every time you treat another person kindly, you're following Jesus' "golden rule."

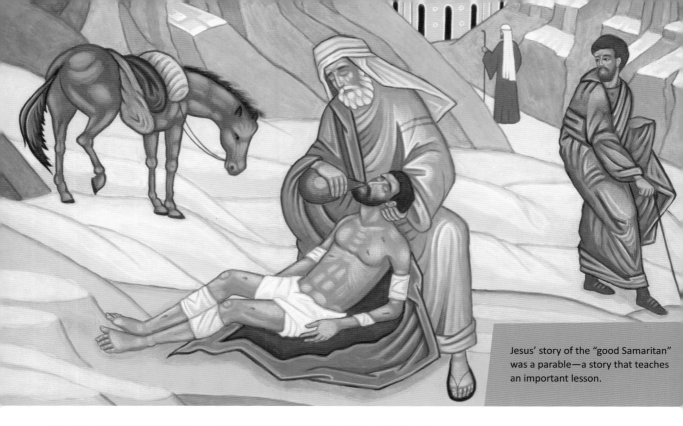

Jesus' story of the "good Samaritan" was a parable—a story that teaches an important lesson.

JESUS' PARABLES: STORIES WITH REAL MEANING

Sometimes when Jesus taught, He just told people what He knew they needed to hear. For example, when He said, "love those who hate you," everyone knew exactly what He meant. Other times, though, Jesus taught by telling stories. These stories are called "parables," and Jesus told a lot of them.

Many times, people remember important lessons when they come in the form of interesting stories. Jesus also knew that the people who really loved Him and wanted to follow Him would listen closely so they could understand the important points of His stories.

Jesus used parables to teach on subjects such as the love and mercy of God, the importance of doing what God says, forgiving other people,

God's eternal kingdom, and how God sees into our hearts.

During His time on earth, Jesus spoke more than forty parables. All of them are important, but here are five of the best-known:

- **Parable of the Good Samaritan (Luke 10:25–37)**—In Jesus' day, Jewish people and Samaritans didn't like each other very much. But in this story, a Samaritan man helped a Jewish man who had been beaten and robbed—and that was after two Jewish religious leaders had passed by the injured man. This story teaches that being a good neighbor means helping everyone who really needs it—even those we might think of as "enemies."

- **Parable of the Unmerciful Servant (Matthew 18:23–35)**—Forgiving other people is a huge deal to God. He wants us to forgive others the same way He's forgiven us. In this story, a king forgave his servant's huge debt, which the servant had no way of paying off. But that same servant soon found a man who owed him a little money and had him thrown in jail because he couldn't pay up. When the king learned what this unmerciful servant did, he demanded full payment of what he owed after all. There was no way the servant could do that.

- **Parable of the Pharisee and the Tax Collector (Luke 18:9–14)**—In Jesus' time, the Jewish people thought tax collectors were the worst people around. They worked for the Roman government, which had control over Israel. And they often collected more than what people owed and kept the extra money for themselves. In this parable, Jesus described a religious leader and a tax collector who went into the temple to pray. The tax collector cried out to God, asking for forgiveness because he knew he had done wrong to many people. But the religious leader was proud, thanking God that he wasn't as bad as the tax collector. Jesus said that the religious leader was *not* forgiven for his sins, while the tax collector was. That's because the tax collector knew he was sinful—he humbled himself and begged God for mercy. The religious leader didn't believe he needed God's forgiveness.

In a parable of Jesus, a Pharisee—a proud religious law-keeper—looks up and says to God, "I thank You that I am not like other men." But a humble tax collector bows before God, saying, "Have pity on me! I am a sinner!" (Luke 18:11, 13).

IT'S IN THE BIBLE!

[Jesus said] "Whoever makes himself look more important than he is will find out how little he is worth. Whoever does not try to honor himself will be made important" (Luke 18:14).

- **Parable of the Wise and Foolish Builders (Matthew 7:24–27)**—With this parable, Jesus taught that it's important for people to build their lives on His teaching. He said people who listened to His words and did what He said were like a man who builds his home on a solid rock foundation, not on soft sand. When we build our lives on Jesus' teaching, He said, problems in life won't make us stop trusting in God or living for Him. But if we don't base our lives on Jesus' words, our problems will cause us to doubt God—we'll look for answers in something other than Him. It's always best to do what Jesus tells us to do.

- **Parable of the Prodigal Son (Luke 15:11–32)**— In this story, a young man asked his father to give him his inheritance early so he could move away from home. The boy went to the city, where he quickly wasted all his money on wild living with new friends. Before long, he didn't even have enough money to buy food, so he went to work for a pig farmer—and the slop he fed the hogs started to look good!

The young man realized that even his father's servants were living better than he did, so he decided to go home and ask his father if he could become a servant himself. But as he got close to his father's home, he noticed his dad running to him! The older man welcomed the boy home—and as a son, not a servant. This story teaches many things about God, but perhaps the most important is that He is very happy to forgive us and welcome us back when we decide to return to Him.

In Jesus' parable of the lost son (also called the parable of the prodigal son), a loving father runs to welcome back the foolish young man who had left his home. The story was a picture of the way God the father welcomes sinful people into His own family.

THE WAY TO ETERNAL LIFE (JOHN 3:1–21)

One evening in Jerusalem, Jesus spoke what is probably the most important thing He ever said. A man named Nicodemus sat down with Jesus to discuss why He had come and what He planned to do. Nicodemus was a Pharisee, one of the Jewish religious leaders who specialized in Old Testament law—also known as the Law of Moses.

Many times, the Pharisees asked Jesus questions to try to trick Him, to trap Him into saying something they could use against Him. At best, they wanted to silence Jesus, but at worst they wanted to do away with Him completely. Nicodemus, though, was different. He asked Jesus questions because he sincerely wanted to know about Him.

Nicodemus didn't believe Jesus was the Messiah the Jews had been waiting for—at least not yet. They expected a powerful king or military leader who would lead the

Jewish people in a revolt against the Roman government. But Jesus was not that kind of leader.

Nicodemus knew about the miracles Jesus had performed, and he might even have listened as Jesus spoke to the crowds of people who followed Him. The Pharisee knew there was something special about this man—he even told Jesus, "Teacher, we know You have come from God to teach us. No one can do these powerful works You do unless God is with Him" (John 3:2).

A Jewish religious leader named Nicodemus was the first person ever to hear what we now call John 3:16: "For God so loved the world that He gave His only Son. Whoever puts his trust in God's Son will not be lost but will have life that lasts forever."

Jesus didn't even acknowledge Nicodemus's statement. He really didn't need to. Both men knew Nicodemus had spoken the truth. Instead, Jesus talked about what gave people a right relationship with God. He told Nicodemus, "For sure, I tell you, unless a man is born again, he cannot see the holy nation of God" (John 3:3).

That didn't make sense to Nicodemus. The idea of being "born again" made him think of something that was not a physical possibility. How in the world could a fully grown man like him go back to his mother's womb? How could he be born all over again? And Nicodemus was probably thinking that he obeyed God's laws and insisted that others did too. That had to make him right with God and earn him a place in the eternal kingdom, didn't it?

Jesus patiently explained what He meant. He told Nicodemus, "For sure, I tell you, unless a man is born of water and of the Spirit of God, he cannot get into the holy nation of God" (John 3:5). Being born again means that the Holy Spirit gives a person a new spiritual life (3:6). Without the Holy Spirit, Jesus said, there is no way to be born again.

As a Pharisee, Nicodemus knew the Old Testament scriptures very well. So Jesus reminded him about a story from the book of Numbers. It was about Moses holding up a bronze snake on a pole so that Israelites who had been bitten by poisonous serpents could be healed. All they had to do was believe God and look at that metal snake.

Jesus then said that He was the Son of Man who had come down from heaven, telling Nicodemus, "As Moses lifted up the snake in the desert, so the Son of Man must be lifted up. Then whoever puts his trust in Him will have life that lasts forever" (John 3:14–15).

But Jesus also told Nicodemus something that each one of us needs to understand. Jesus had come to save people from their sins—it had nothing to do with anything good Nicodemus or any of us

Every human being is "born of water" (John 3:5), from the fluid inside the mother's womb. But Jesus said being "born again" comes through God's Spirit.

had done or ever would do. Salvation was all about what Jesus was going to do. He summed up the message of His Gospel like this:

"For God so loved the world that He gave His only Son. Whoever puts his trust in God's Son will not be lost but will have life that lasts forever. For God did not send His Son into the world to say it is guilty. He sent His Son so the world might be saved from the punishment of sin by Him."

JOHN 3:16–17

Jesus knew He would one day be "lifted up" so that people could be saved through Him—He would be lifted up on a wooden cross. This was His most important mission: to take the punishment for our sins. By believing in Jesus' death and resurrection, we gain good standing with God. We become members of His family while we live here on earth, and we know we will always be with Him through eternity.

As you read Chapters 7 and 8 of this book, you'll learn more details of Jesus' death and the way God brought Him back to life.

WHO SAID THAT?

"How can a man be born when he is old? How can he get into his mother's body and be born the second time?" (John 3:4).

A man named Nicodemus asked Jesus this question one evening in Jerusalem. Nicodemus was a religious leader during Jesus' time on earth. He also played a part in Jesus' burial after He had died on the cross. (You can read about that in John 19:39–42.)

PART III

WHEN EVERYTHING CHANGED

In the past four chapters, you read about Jesus' birth and childhood, the things He did and the places He visited, and the lessons He taught. All of those things are important parts of Jesus' story. But every one of them was building up to His ultimate purpose for coming to earth.

From the time Jesus started His ministry, He knew it would end with His terrible death on a cross. But Jesus' crucifixion wouldn't really be the end—on the third day after His death, God would bring Him back to life! After that, Jesus would stay on earth for forty days. Many people would see Him, then go tell others that He was alive again—just as He had promised.

After those forty days, Jesus went back to His Father in heaven. But He left behind a group of followers who would continue preaching His message of salvation from sin. Jesus knew these men couldn't do this hard work all by themselves, so He promised to send a "Helper"—the Holy Spirit of God. And about a week after Jesus returned to heaven, He kept that promise. On the special day called Pentecost the Holy Spirit filled everyone who followed Jesus—and the apostles became courageous preachers who would change the whole world.

In the next three chapters, you'll read about Jesus' final days on earth—His arrival in Jerusalem, His arrest and trial, and His death and resurrection. Not only that, you'll read about the amazing things His original apostles (as well as some other believers) did in the years after Jesus returned to heaven.

When you put all these things together, you have the incredible story of how much God loves us.

Jesus' death on the cross was sad but necessary. His resurrection—coming back to life—is the happy part of the story: This stained glass window shows Jesus, alive again and pointing out His wounds from the crucifixion!

CHAPTER 7

SOME FINAL PREPARATIONS

IN THIS CHAPTER:

- Jesus' final entry into Jerusalem
- Religious leaders oppose Jesus during "Holy Week"
- Jesus' farewell to the disciples at the "Last Supper"
- Jesus arrested in the Garden of Gethsemane

For about three years, Jesus traveled around Israel doing good for people. He taught them, encouraged them, healed them, and fed them. But He knew His ultimate mission was still ahead of Him.

Jesus had always known that He would go to Jerusalem to die on a cross, then be raised from the dead. He began to prepare His apostles for His death when they were visiting a place called Caesarea Philippi. But here's what the Bible says happened soon afterward:

From that time on Jesus began to tell His followers that He had to go to Jerusalem and suffer many things. These hard things would come from the leaders and from the head religious leaders of the Jews and from the teachers of the Law. He told them He would be killed and three days later He would be raised from the dead.
MATTHEW 16:21

Peter didn't like what Jesus was saying, and took the Lord aside to "correct" Him.

"Never, Lord!" Peter said. "This must not happen to You!" (Matthew 16:22). But Jesus scolded Peter back, even more strongly: "Get behind Me, Satan! You are standing in My way. You are not thinking how God thinks. You are thinking how man thinks" (Matthew 16:23).

Peter thought he was doing good by scolding Jesus. After all, none of the apostles wanted Jesus to die on a cross! But at that time in Jesus' ministry, Peter and the others didn't fully understand why Jesus had come to earth. But Jesus did, and that's why He responded so strongly to Peter.

Then, not long before Jesus went to Jerusalem for the last time, He told His apostles:

"Listen! We are going up to Jerusalem. The Son of Man will be handed over to the religious leaders and to the teachers of the Law. They will say that He must be put to death. They will hand Him over to the people who do not know God. They will make fun of Him and will beat Him. They will nail Him to a cross. Three days later He will be raised to life."
MATTHEW 20:18–19

After hearing Jesus' words, the apostles probably wanted to go anywhere but Jerusalem. But they had faithfully followed Jesus for three years, so they followed Him now too.

A HUGE CELEBRATION (MATTHEW 21:1–11, MARK 11:1–11, LUKE 19:29–44, JOHN 12:12–19)

Around five hundred years before Jesus came to earth, God sent a message describing the way the Messiah would enter the city of Jerusalem for the last time. The Old Testament prophet Zechariah wrote, "Be full of joy, O people of Zion! Call out in a loud voice, O people of Jerusalem! See, your King is coming to you. He is fair and good and has the power to save. He is not proud and sits on a donkey, on the son of a female donkey" (Zechariah 9:9).

Every year, Christians from around the world gather in Jerusalem to remember the first Palm Sunday, when people laid their coats and palm branches on the road to make a path for Jesus.

There would be celebration in the streets of Jerusalem as the humble Jesus rode into the city. People had been waiting for many years for their Messiah—and though they didn't understand everything about the Savior's work, they knew Jesus was that Man.

Near the towns of Bethpage and Bethany, Jesus and His disciples prepared for His final entry into Jerusalem. Jesus told two of His followers to go to a village and get a young donkey for Him to ride. If anyone asked them why they were taking the animal, Jesus said to tell them, "The Lord needs it. He will send it back again soon" (Mark 11:3).

The two men walked to the village and found a mother donkey and her colt tied to a post on the street, just as Jesus had told them. They repeated what Jesus had instructed them to say to the people who asked what they were doing. Then they returned to Jesus and the other disciples. The disciples put their coats on the donkey's back, and Jesus sat on the young animal. It was time for what is called the "Triumphal Entry" into Jerusalem.

IT'S IN THE BIBLE!

When Jesus came into Jerusalem, all the people of the city were troubled. They said, "Who is this?" Many people said, "This is Jesus, the One Who speaks for God from the town of Nazareth in the country of Galilee" (Matthew 21:10-11).

It was the week before the Jews' Passover celebration. Thousands of visitors from all over the world were in Jerusalem to celebrate and worship God. As Jesus entered the city, people lined the roadway. Some spread their coats on the road ahead of Jesus, and others cut branches from palm trees to place on the road. (When Christians today remember the time Jesus entered Jerusalem, they call it "Palm Sunday.")

People crowded around Jesus as He made His way up the street. They were shouting, "Praise God for the Son of David! Blessings on the one who comes in the name of the LORD! Praise God in highest heaven!" (Matthew 21:9 NLT).

In many Bible versions, the words "Praise God" in Matthew 21:9 appear as *Hosanna*, a Hebrew word that means "oh, save!" in English. When the people cheered for Jesus on His way into the city, they thought they were welcoming a powerful king—one who would free them from Roman rule. Jesus did come to save them, but not from the Romans. He came to free them—and us—from sin.

JESUS' FINAL DAYS IN JERUSALEM

Many churches commemorate the days between Jesus' Triumphal Entry into Jerusalem and His resurrection as "Holy Week." It was a very dramatic time for Jesus

He spent those days traveling back and forth between Bethany (where His friends Lazarus, Mary, and Martha lived) and Jerusalem, teaching, performing miracles, and preparing His disciples for what would happen to Him (and to them) as the week went on.

The Triumphal Entry took place on the first day of the week. While Monday is usually our first day of work or school each week, Sunday is actually the first day of the week. When Jesus entered Jerusalem, He went to the temple where He became very angry—people were buying and selling animals for the Passover sacrifices right in the place that they should have been worshiping God. Jesus chased the merchants out of the temple, turned over their tables, and shouted, "It is written, 'My house is to be called a house of prayer.' You have made it a place of robbers" (Matthew 21:13).

WHAT DOES THIS MEAN TO ME?

"For sure, I tell you this: If you have faith and do not doubt, you will not only be able to do what was done to the fig tree. You will also be able to say to this mountain, 'Move from here and be thrown into the sea,' and it will be done. All things you ask for in prayer, you will receive if you have faith" (Matthew 21:21–22).

Jesus wanted His followers to understand the importance of believing that God *wanted* to answer their prayers. What do you believe God wants to do for you today? When you ask for good things with faith, He'll do them for you!

Here is a side of Jesus that surprises many people—His anger over the misuse of God's temple, and the way He threw the greedy merchants out.

After this—what some people call "Jesus cleansing the temple"—He stayed for a while to heal the blind and lame people who came to Him for help. The religious leaders and teachers saw what He was doing, and they heard children looking toward the temple and calling out to Jesus, "Greatest One! Son of David!" (Matthew 21:15). These men had never liked Jesus, and they were very angry at what the kids were saying. So they complained to Jesus, "Do you hear what these children are saying?" The religious leaders wanted Jesus to stop the children, but instead He said, "Yes, have you not read the writings, 'Even little children and babies will honor Him'?" (Matthew 21:16).

After His visit to the temple, Jesus left Jerusalem and went to spend the night with His apostles in Bethany. But for the rest of the week, the Jewish religious leaders looked for reasons to arrest Jesus and have Him killed.

Sometimes the religious leaders tried to trick Jesus with difficult questions about the Old Testament law. But He always had an answer for them. One day, an expert in the law asked Jesus,

"Teacher, which one is the greatest of the laws?" The religious leaders hoped they could accuse Jesus of disrespecting the rest of the Law by saying one rule was most important. But Jesus quickly answered:

" 'You must love the Lord your God with all your heart and with all your soul and with all your mind.' This is the first and greatest of the Laws. The second is like it, 'You must love your neighbor as you love yourself.' All the Laws and the writings of the early preachers depend on these two most important Laws."
MATTHEW 22:37–40

Jesus then asked the religious leaders a tough question that they couldn't answer (see Matthew 22:41–46). They stopped asking Him questions—but they kept trying to find ways to accuse and arrest Him.

THE PLOT TO KILL JESUS (MATTHEW 26:1-5, 14-16; MARK 14:1-2, 10-11; LUKE 22:1-6)

Even though Jesus was a good man who did many good things for others, some people in positions of authority wanted to kill Him. They didn't believe that God had a Son, so they hated it when Jesus claimed to be the Son of God. Jesus knew that the leaders were plotting against Him, but He also knew those things were part of God's plan.

A few days before Passover, Jesus reminded the disciples that He was going to die soon. He would be crucified, one of the worst possible ways to die. Meanwhile, the religious leaders in Jerusalem were meeting at the home of Caiaphas, the top Jewish leader in Jerusalem.

There, they hatched a plot to have Jesus arrested and killed.

But it turned out that these men would have help from one of Jesus' own followers. Judas Iscariot slipped away from the disciples and approached the chief priests. He asked them what they would give him to hand over Jesus. The chief priests counted out thirty pieces of silver and sent Judas away. Then he waited for the opportunity to betray Jesus.

Jesus knew what Judas was doing. But He didn't stop the betrayal, because even Judas's terrible choice was part of God's plan to save people from their sin.

Judas Iscariot, at left, considers the Jewish priests' offer of thirty pieces of silver in exchange for leading them to Jesus.

IN THE "UPPER ROOM" (MATTHEW 26:17-35, MARK 14:12-31, LUKE 22:7-38, JOHN 13)

Jesus knew His time with the apostles was short, so He called them together for one final meal as a group. They met in an upstairs room of a house in Jerusalem. Many Bible experts believe this "upper room" belonged to the family of a young man named John Mark, who would later write the Gospel of Mark.

With all twelve apostles gathered around Him, Jesus began by showing them something very important. He knew that the Twelve had been arguing among themselves about which one of them was the most important (Luke 22:24). That was the wrong attitude for them to have, so Jesus showed His disciples what humbleness looked like.

Jesus got up from the table, then found a pan and filled it with water. Soon, He was washing and drying the apostles' feet, a job usually done by servants. Jesus wanted the men to understand that they should serve one another and think of others as more important than themselves. Then He told them:

"I am your Teacher and Lord. I have washed your feet. You should wash each other's feet also. I have done this to show you what should be done. You should do as I have done to you. For sure, I tell you, a workman who is owned by someone is not greater than his owner. One who is sent is not greater than the one who sent him. If you know these things, you will be happy if you do them."
JOHN 13:14-17

Later, as the apostles were eating, Jesus made a shocking announcement: "I tell you the truth, one of you will betray me" (Matthew 26:21 NLT). The apostles looked around at each other, wondering who would do something so terrible. But Jesus knew it would be Judas, a man whose feet He had just washed. Judas had already taken money to give Jesus up to the authorities, so he got up quickly and left the room.

Jesus washes His disciples' feet—a job usually done by a household servant—to set an example of humility that every Christian should follow.

IT'S IN THE BIBLE!

[Jesus said,] "I give you a new Law. You are to love each other. You must love each other as I have loved you. If you love each other, all men will know you are My followers" (John 13:34-35).

As part of the meal, Jesus took bread, gave thanks for it, and broke it. Then He gave each disciple a piece, telling them, "Take, eat, this is My body" (Matthew 26:26). He also took a cup of wine and told the men, "You must all drink from it. This is My blood of the New Way of Worship which is given for many. It is given so the sins of many can be forgiven" (Matthew 26:27–28).

SOME LAST-MINUTE INSTRUCTIONS (JOHN 14–16)

In a matter of hours, Jesus would die on a cross to provide a way for people to be forgiven of their sins. Now that He had gathered His apostles together for their last meal, Jesus gave them some final teaching. (You can read what He said in John 14–16. . .it's good stuff!)

Jesus started with comforting words: "Do not let your heart be troubled. You have put your trust in God, put your trust in Me also" (John 14:1). He assured the disciples that after He had returned to heaven, He would prepare a place where they could live with God forever.

Jesus also taught them some very important things. He said they should love God first and not love the world. He also told them, "Your hearts are full of sorrow because I am telling you these things. I tell you the truth. It is better for you that I go away. If I do not go, the Helper will not come to you. If I go, I will send Him to you" (John 16:6–7).

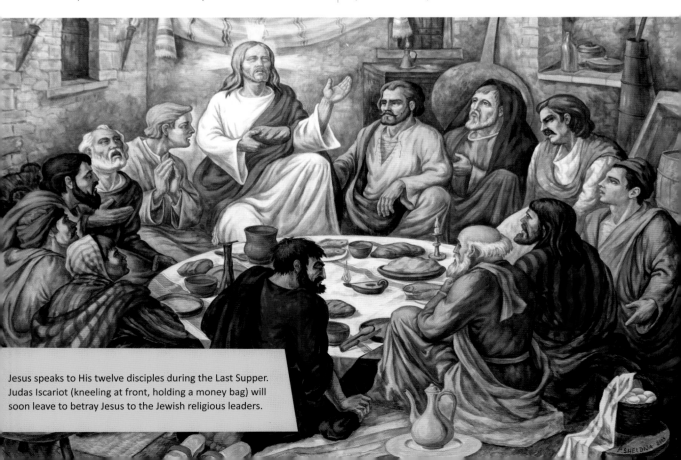

Jesus speaks to His twelve disciples during the Last Supper. Judas Iscariot (kneeling at front, holding a money bag) will soon leave to betray Jesus to the Jewish religious leaders.

IT'S IN THE BIBLE!

[Jesus said,] "For sure, I tell you, whoever puts his trust in Me can do the things I am doing. He will do even greater things than these because I am going to the Father. Whatever you ask in My name, I will do it so the shining-greatness of the Father may be seen in the Son" (John 14:12–13).

in His moment of greatest need. Peter didn't believe that, and told Jesus that he would never abandon his Lord. But Jesus told Peter that before the night was over—before the rooster crowed to signal the new day—he would deny three times that he even knew Jesus. Peter was very sad when he heard this, and he and the rest of the apostles promised they would never leave Jesus, even if it meant dying for Him that night.

The "Helper" Jesus mentioned was the Holy Spirit, who would come to the disciples weeks later. Jesus told the eleven remaining apostles (remember, Judas Iscariot had left the group) that the Holy Spirit would remind them of the things He had taught them. The Spirit would also show people that they needed God's forgiveness for their sins and lead them to Jesus. You'll learn more about the Holy Spirit's arrival in Chapter 9 of this book.

That night, the apostles would see Jesus arrested. But before they left to go to Jerusalem, Jesus prayed for Himself, for His apostles, and for every other Christian who would ever live. (If you want to see for yourself how much Jesus loves you, read that prayer in John 17.)

After dinner, Jesus and the apostles sang a song of praise to God. Then they left for a garden called Gethsemane. On the way there, Jesus told the disciples that they would all be ashamed of Him during His arrest. They would desert Him

The apostle Peter pledges his loyalty to Jesus, no matter what. Sadly, Peter couldn't keep his promise—but Jesus would forgive him. (Why is Peter holding a key? See Matthew 16:18–19.)

The garden of Gethsemane today. In this general spot, just before He was betrayed by Judas Iscariot, Jesus prayed. Then He was arrested and carried away to a trial.

ARRESTED LIKE A COMMON CRIMINAL (MATTHEW 26:36–56, MARK 14:32–52, LUKE 22:32–51, JOHN 18:1–13)

Jesus and the apostles walked through the Kidron Valley to the Mount of Olives, a place near the eastern side of Jerusalem. They went to an olive garden there called Gethsemane. Jesus told the apostles, "You sit here while I go over there to pray" (Matthew 26:36).

Then Jesus took His three closest friends—Peter, James, and John—and walked a short distance away from the other apostles. He told the three, "My soul is very sad. My soul is so full of sorrow I am ready to die. You stay here and watch with Me" (Matthew 26:38). He also told them, "Pray that you will not be tempted" (Luke 22:40). Jesus walked a short distance farther by Himself, fell to His face, and began to pray.

Jesus knew what was ahead for Him—terrible pain, sadness, and loneliness. His human side wanted more than anything to find another way. So He prayed, "Father, if it can be done, take away what must happen to Me." But He knew the hard things were part of God's plan, so He said, "Even so, not what I want, but what You want" (Luke 22:42).

Jesus had told Peter, James, and John to stay behind and pray, but they fell asleep. When Jesus had finished His own praying, He woke them up and told Peter, "Were you not able to watch with Me one hour? Watch and pray so that you will not be tempted. Man's spirit is willing, but the body does not have the power to do it" (Matthew 26:40–41).

Jesus went back to pray in private. Again He pleaded with God, asking if there wasn't another way to bring salvation to the people of the world. "My Father," He prayed, "if this must happen to Me, may whatever You want be done" (Matthew 26:42).

When Jesus returned to the apostles, they were asleep again! He went back to His private place a third time to pray. He was hurting so bad inside that sweat fell from His forehead like big drops of blood. The Bible says that God the Father sent an angel to encourage Jesus. When He returned to the apostles, He woke them up again and said, "Are you still sleeping and getting your rest? As I speak, the time has come when the Son of Man will be handed over to sinners. Get up and let us go. See! The man who will hand Me over is near" (Matthew 26:45–46).

Just then, Judas arrived, leading a crowd of Jewish religious leaders and Roman soldiers. Some of them carried clubs and swords and some carried torches. Judas walked up to Jesus and kissed Him on the cheek, a sign to let the mob know who to arrest. Jesus looked Judas in

Judas Iscariot leads Jewish religious leaders and a band of armed men to arrest Jesus. Notice Peter at lower right, drawing his sword on a man named Malchus.

the eye and asked him, "Judas, are you handing over the Son of Man with a kiss?" (Luke 22:48).

Jesus was prepared for what was about to happen. He asked the soldiers who they were looking for, and they answered, "Jesus of Nazareth." "I am Jesus," He told them. At the sound of His name, the crowd fell backwards for a moment. But they regrouped and surrounded Jesus again. He asked the mob to let His followers leave before they arrested Him (see John 18:4–9).

When Peter realized what was happening, he tried to defend Jesus. He pulled out his sword and started swinging it wildly at the men who had come to take Jesus away. Peter apparently wasn't a very skilled swordsman (remember, he'd always been a fisherman)—but he caught a man named Malchus, a servant of the Jewish high priest, on the side of the head and sliced off his ear. Jesus scolded Peter, and then touched the man's ear and healed his wound. Jesus then told Peter:

"Put your sword back where it belongs.
Everyone who uses a sword will die with
a sword. Do you not think that I can pray
to My Father? At once He would send Me
more than 70,000 angels. If I did, how
could it happen as the Holy Writings said
it would happen? It must be this way."
MATTHEW 26:52–54

Jesus knew and perfectly understood something that the apostles didn't. He had told them several times that He would die and then be raised from the dead, but they never really "got it." That's why Jesus told them right then that He was going to let these things happen. God could have stopped what occurred in the Garden of Gethsemane, but Jesus' arrest was a part of His plan—and He wasn't going to change that.

Jesus was tied up and led away. The apostles, terrified and heartbroken, ran away, just as Jesus had said they would. Only two—Peter and John—followed Him at a safe distance. For the next several hours, Jesus would be alone as He faced trial by the religious leaders and the Roman authorities. . .and after that, execution.

CHAPTER 8

JESUS' ULTIMATE MISSION

IN THIS CHAPTER:

- Jesus on trial
- Jesus condemned to die
- Jesus' death on a cross
- Jesus' resurrection
- The risen Jesus appears to His followers

We can only imagine the pain and disappointment Jesus' apostles—as well as the rest of His followers—must have felt after their Teacher and Lord had been arrested in the Garden of Gethsemane.

They had followed Him for three years, learning from Him and being amazed at the things He did for other people. He had told them that He was going to be arrested and then handed over to the Romans to be crucified. But somehow that message never sank in.

In their minds, it just wasn't supposed to end like this!

The story of Jesus' life on earth would have a wonderful, world-changing end. But before that happened, things would get worse—a *lot* worse—for the people who followed Him. Soon, however, their heartache and disappointment would be turned into the joy of knowing that Jesus had defeated death.

In this chapter, you'll read about Jesus' most important mission here on earth: to die a terrible death on a Roman cross before God the Father brought Him back from the dead. We'll start that part of Jesus' story with the trial—make that the *trials*—He would endure before He went to the cross.

A woman visits the "prison of Christ" in Jerusalem. Some believe Jesus stayed here before He went in front of the Roman governor, Pilate.

JESUS ON TRIAL (MATTHEW 26:57-27:10, MARK 14:53-15:20, LUKE 22:54-23:24, JOHN 18:13-19:3)

After Jesus' arrest in the garden, the mob of soldiers and Jewish religious leaders took Him to a man named Annas. He was the father-in-law of the top Jewish priest in Jerusalem at the time—in the Bible, this man is called the "high priest." Annas had been the Jewish high priest in the past, and he still had a lot of power and authority at the time He met with Jesus.

Annas asked Jesus about His followers and the things He had taught. But Jesus told him, "I have spoken very plain words to the world. I have always taught in the Jewish place of worship and in the house of God. It is where the Jews go all the time. My words have not been said in secret. Why do you ask Me? Ask those who have heard what I said to them. They know what I said" (John 18:20–21).

Then a soldier standing nearby slapped Jesus. He said, "Is that how You talk to the head religious leaders?" But Jesus told him, "If I said anything wrong, tell Me what was wrong. If I said what was right, why did you hit Me? (John 19:22–23).

Annas had heard enough to know that the religious leaders would want to put Jesus on trial. So he sent Jesus to Caiaphas, the current high priest. All the religious leaders and teachers gathered at Caiaphas's home to put Jesus on trial.

Caiaphas questioned Jesus, but He didn't answer. . .until the priest asked Him, "Are You the Christ, the Son of the Holy One?" (Mark 14:61). Jesus answered him, "I am! And you will see the Son of Man seated on the right side of the All-powerful God. You will see Him coming again in the clouds of the sky" (verse 62).

Jesus stands on trial before the Jewish religious leaders. They will call for His death.

That was all Caiaphas needed to hear. He tore his clothes, which was a Jewish way of showing extreme anger or sadness over something. "Do we need other people to speak against Him?" he asked the others in the room. "You have heard Him speak as if He were God! What do you think?" (Mark 14:63–64).

The religious leaders declared Jesus guilty of blasphemy—they said He was insulting God by claiming to *be* God. They spit on Jesus, covered His face and hit Him and then made fun of Him, saying "Tell us what is going to happen" (Mark 14:65). Even the soldiers hit Jesus as they led Him away and took Him to the palace of Pontius Pilate, the Roman governor of Judea.

At some point, while the religious leaders were questioning Jesus, Peter was in the courtyard of the high priest's home, watching what was happening. A young woman recognized Peter and said to him, "This man was with Jesus also." But Peter, fearing for his own life, told her, "Woman, I do not know Him" (Luke 22:57). Peter headed toward the gate, but someone else recognized Him as one of Jesus' followers and said, "You are one of them also," but Peter said, "No, sir, I am not" (verse 58). Not long after that, someone else in the crowd said him, "For sure, this man was with Jesus also because he is from Galilee." But Peter said, "Sir, I do not know what you are saying" (verses 59–60). Immediately, Peter heard a rooster crowing. Just then, Jesus was passing by and looked directly at Peter. The apostle remembered that Jesus had predicted he would deny knowing the Lord three times. Peter went outside the courtyard gates and cried in shame.

A rooster, at upper left, gets ready to crow as Peter—warming himself by the fire—says he doesn't know Jesus.

Pilate, the Roman governor in Jerusalem, didn't believe Jesus had done anything wrong. But he gave in to the demands of the Jewish leaders and allowed Jesus to be crucified.

TRIED BY ROMAN AUTHORITIES

The Jewish religious leaders knew they could not execute anyone, even if they found a person guilty of blasphemy. Only the Roman government could kill a criminal. So they took Jesus to Pontius Pilate, the Roman governor of Judea.

When the religious leaders approached Pilate, he asked them what they were accusing Jesus of doing. They told the governor that Jesus claimed to be a king. They knew that claiming to be a king would be a serious challenge to the Roman government. When Pilate asked Jesus if He was the King of the Jews, Jesus answered, "My holy nation is not of this world" (John 18:36).

Pilate told the religious leaders that he didn't find Jesus guilty of anything. When they heard that, they became even more angry. So they said, "He makes trouble among the people. He has been teaching over all the country of Judea, starting in Galilee and now here" (Luke 23:5).

When Pilate heard the word *Galilee*, he decided to send Jesus to Herod Antipas, the son of Herod the Great, who was ruling the province of Galilee. Herod happened to be in Jerusalem at the time. He had heard of Jesus and the miracles He had done in Galilee, so Herod was glad to see Jesus in person. He hoped Jesus would even perform miracles for him, but when he asked Jesus questions, the Lord was silent.

Though Jesus didn't answer Herod's questions—and though the religious leaders kept saying false things about Him—Herod didn't find any reason to execute Jesus either. Herod and his soldiers said mean things to Jesus, and they put a robe on Him to make fun of His claim to be a king. But Herod sent Jesus back to Pilate.

"I have sinned because I handed over a Man Who has done no wrong" (Matthew 27:4).

When Judas, one of Jesus' twelve apostles, learned that Jesus was on trial for His life, he felt very guilty. Judas went to the religious leaders who were plotting to have Jesus killed and tried to return the thirty pieces of silver he had received for betraying Jesus. When the religious leaders wouldn't hear him, Judas went out and killed himself.

The governor of Judea didn't want to crucify Jesus. Not only did he believe Jesus was innocent, he'd received a message from his wife that said, "Have nothing to do with that good Man. I have been troubled today in a dream about Him" (Matthew 27:19).

Pilate called the religious leaders and teachers and other people to meet with him outside his palace. He told the crowd that he hadn't found Jesus guilty of anything deserving death. Pilate was hoping to let Him go free.

The governor tried again to keep Jesus from crucifixion. He had Jesus stand in front of the Jewish religious leaders and again tried to persuade them to let Him to go free.

But the mob shouted back to Pilate, "If you let this Man go free, you are not a friend of Caesar! Whoever makes himself as a king is working against Caesar" (John 19:12). Pilate knew that the Jewish leaders could cause him big problems if they reported him to the Roman emperor, Tiberius Claudius Nero. But Pilate tried one last time to find a way to have Jesus set free.

Barabbas scuffles with his Roman guards, in a reenactment of the story of Jesus' trial and crucifixion. Barabbas was in prison for revolting against the government and for murder—but the Jewish religious leaders preferred him over Jesus.

It was tradition to release one prisoner during the Passover celebration. So Pilate brought out a known robber and murderer named Barabbas. Pilate believed the crowd would rather have Barabbas put to death than Jesus. But he was wrong.

"Which one of the two do you want me to let go free?" Pilate asked, and the crowd shouted out "Barabbas!" (Matthew 27:21). Pilate was out of ideas to free Jesus. When he asked the crowd one last time what He should do with Jesus, the people all said, "Nail Him to a cross!" (verse 23).

So Pilate gave in to the crowd's demands. But first, he brought out a basin filled with water and washed his hands in front of the people. He told the crowd, "I am not guilty of the blood of this good Man. This is your own doing" (Matthew 27:24). The crowd answered, "Let His blood be on us and on our children!" (verse 25).

Before He was crucified, Jesus was punished by flogging. At that time, criminals were often punished by being flogged or "scourged." This was a terrible beating with a whip made of leather straps, with metal balls or sharp pieces of bone braided into the leather.

In the Old Testament, God had commanded that no Israelite receive more than forty lashes. The Jews had cut off the punishment at thirty-nine lashes, to keep from accidentally breaking the law. But the Romans weren't limited to the Jewish law. The Bible doesn't say how many times they whipped Jesus, but these beatings were sometimes so bad that they caused a criminal to die before he could be crucified. Jesus was probably close to dying even before He went to the cross. But He was still alive, and that's because He hadn't yet finished the job God had for Him to do.

WHO SAID THAT?

"You brought this Man to me as one that leads the people in the wrong way. I have asked Him about these things in front of you. I do not find Him guilty of the things you say against Him" (Luke 23:14).

Pontius Pilate, the Roman governor of Judea in the land of Israel, said this to Jesus' accusers. When they wouldn't listen, Pilate gave in to their demands and ordered that Jesus be crucified.

Pontius Pilate washes his hands, a way of saying he didn't take responsibility for sending Jesus to the cross. He didn't want to crucify Jesus, but let the angry Jewish leaders have their way.

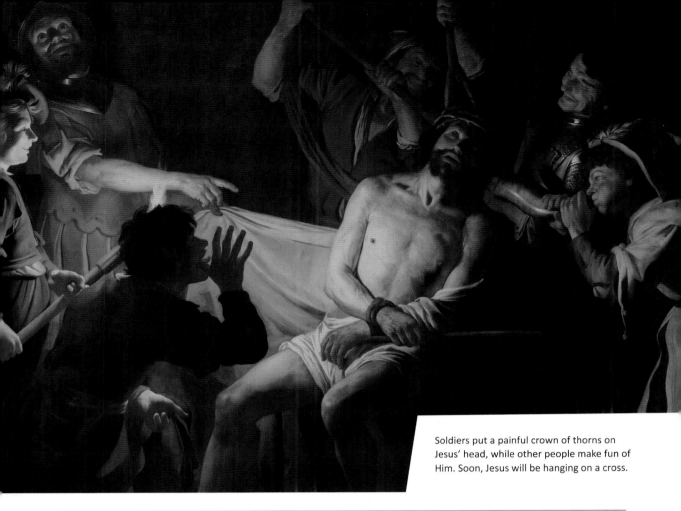

Soldiers put a painful crown of thorns on Jesus' head, while other people make fun of Him. Soon, Jesus will be hanging on a cross.

JESUS' DEATH ON A CROSS (MATTHEW 27:27–54, MARK 15:15–39, LUKE 23:26–49, JOHN 19:17–37)

After Pilate reluctantly sent Jesus off to be crucified, Roman soldiers took Him to their headquarters and put a purple robe on Him. They made a crown of thorns and put it on His head and then put a stick in His hand like a king's scepter. They were just making fun of Him, and saying things like, "Hail! King of the Jews!" (Matthew 27:29 NLT). They spit on Jesus and then hit Him on the head with a stick.

When the soldiers got tired of mocking Jesus, they took Him out to crucify Him. They made Him carry His own cross toward a place just outside the city of Jerusalem called "the Place of the Skull." It was also known as Golgotha, or Calvary.

Along the way, the soldiers forced a man named Simon to carry Jesus' cross. Simon was from a place in northern Africa called Cyrene, and he was probably in Jerusalem for Passover. Some believe that the soldiers forced Simon to help because Jesus was too weak—He had been beaten so badly that He didn't have the strength to carry the cross all the way by Himself.

CHAPTER 9

SOME FOLKS GOD USED TO CHANGE THE WORLD

IN THIS CHAPTER:

- God sends the Holy Spirit
- Peter's sermon in Jerusalem
- Peter and John preach the Gospel
- The church in Jerusalem grows
- The apostle Paul and his travels

After Jesus' death and resurrection, He told His apostles, "Go and make followers of all the nations. Baptize them in the name of the Father and of the Son and of the Holy Spirit. Teach them to do all the things I have told you" (Matthew 28:19–20).

The first four books of the New Testament (Matthew, Mark, Luke, and John, also known as the Gospels) tell the story of Jesus' life, death, and resurrection. The fifth New Testament book, Acts—sometimes called the Acts of the Apostles—tells the story of how Jesus' followers did as He had instructed them. They took His message of salvation to other parts of the world, starting a movement that changed history.

In Acts 1, you can read about Jesus' final instructions to His apostles. Most Bible experts believe Jesus gave these instructions at the same time He told them to go into the world and make new followers.

Jesus told His disciples, "Do not leave Jerusalem. Wait for what the Father has promised. You heard Me speak of this. For John the Baptist baptized with water but in a few days you will be baptized with the Holy Spirit" (Acts 1:4–5).

The apostles obeyed. They hung out in Jerusalem and waited for God to send His Holy Spirit to them. While they waited, they prayed and chose a man named Matthias to take Judas Iscariot's place as an apostle.

Then God sent the Holy Spirit. It was an amazing scene in Jerusalem!

Jesus' return to heaven—the "Ascension"—meant the Holy Spirit would soon come to live in believers' hearts. . .and help them change the world.

AN AMAZING DAY IN JERUSALEM (ACTS 2)

Before His death on the cross, Jesus told His followers, "Get your life from Me. Then I will live in you and you will give much fruit. You can do nothing without Me" (John 15:5). Jesus knew that His followers couldn't do what He wanted them to do just by their own power. On their own, they couldn't keep following Him and His teaching, and they wouldn't be bold enough to tell others about Him. Jesus had given them a tough assignment, and they needed His help if they were going to make it. That's why He promised to send the Holy Spirit. . .and why He fulfilled that promise not long after He went back to heaven.

On a Jewish holy day called Pentecost, 120 of Jesus' followers were gathered together in Jerusalem. Before He returned to heaven, Jesus had told them to stay there. In this place, and on this day, God would keep Jesus' promise by sending the Holy Spirit.

They probably never guessed it would be such a spectacular event!

The Holy Spirit, represented by the white dove, comes to earth to fill Jesus' followers on the special holiday called Pentecost. The little flames above each person are part of the miraculous event.

IT'S IN THE BIBLE!

[Jesus said,] "But you will receive power when the Holy Spirit comes into your life. You will tell about Me in the city of Jerusalem and over all the countries of Judea and Samaria and to the ends of the earth" (Acts 1:8).

As the people waited, they heard what sounded like a loud, powerful wind. It was so loud that people outside the house could hear it! Then what looked like flames of fire came down and touched each one of them. They were all filled with God's Holy Spirit, and now they were speaking in languages they didn't even know!

All the activity caught the attention of the people in Jerusalem—those who lived in the city, as well as those who were just visiting for the celebration of Pentecost. The visitors were from many other areas, and they spoke different languages—but then they heard these Spirit-filled Christians speaking in their own languages! Nobody knew what to make of it. Some people decided to make fun of these believers, saying they'd had too much wine to drink.

But the apostle Peter, filled with the Holy Spirit, told the crowds that these Christians hadn't been drinking. Peter said that the people in Jerusalem were eyewitnesses to the fulfillment of a promise God made through the Old Testament prophet Joel—that He would one day send His Holy Spirit to live inside people.

But that wasn't all Peter told the people in Jerusalem. Far from it!

Here is Peter, sculpted from rock. Jesus gave Him the name Cephas, which means "rock."

PETER: A CHANGED MAN

In Chapter 8 of this book, you read about the apostle Peter—one of Jesus' twelve closest followers—saying three times that he didn't even know the Lord. That fearful reaction to Jesus' arrest was just one of Peter's failings. When you read the four Gospels, you see that Peter often said and did the wrong things during the three years he followed Jesus' earthly ministry. Peter may have meant well, but that didn't always show in his words or actions.

That was Peter *before* God sent him (and all the other believers) the Holy Spirit. But *after* the Holy Spirit came, Peter was almost a completely different person. You can see how much he had changed in his very first sermon, which is recorded in Acts 2:25–41.

What a sermon it was!

Peter knew that some things he said in that sermon could get him into a lot of trouble with the religious leaders in Jerusalem. After all, those same things had gotten Jesus executed. But the Holy Spirit had given Peter amazing courage—plus the ability to remember exactly what Jesus had said to him and the other apostles.

Peter told a big crowd of people in Jerusalem that Jesus proved He was the Messiah through the things He said and did on earth—and by the fact that God raised Him from the dead. He also said that everyone could see how God had kept Jesus' promise to send the Holy Spirit to live in believers. The evidence was all around them, on that very day.

IT'S IN THE BIBLE!

[The Jews] said to Peter and to the other missionaries, "Brothers, what should we do?" Peter said to them, "Be sorry for your sins and turn from them and be baptized in the name of Jesus Christ, and your sins will be forgiven. You will receive the gift of the Holy Spirit" (Acts 2:37–38).

In an old Italian painting, Peter preaches to a small crowd. It would have been tough to paint the crowd he preached to on the day of Pentecost—enough for three thousand of them to believe in Jesus!

Peter's preaching was so powerful that it touched the hearts of many Jewish people in Jerusalem. That day, *three thousand* of them believed in Jesus and were baptized!

Amazing results, don't you think, for a former fisherman who didn't know when to talk and when to keep his mouth closed?

But that wasn't all Peter did. He remembered that Jesus had told him and the other apostles, "For sure, I tell you, whoever puts his trust in Me can do the things I am doing. He will do even greater things than these because I am going to the Father" (John 14:12). Well, Jesus did go to His Father in heaven, and Peter did do many of the great things he had seen Jesus do. He preached powerfully and he healed sick people, just as Jesus had.

As with Jesus, Peter made some enemies as he preached, taught, and healed people. A lot of people didn't like the things Peter and his friends were saying and doing, and they tried to stop him. They even threatened to put him in prison. But Peter wouldn't stop telling the good news of salvation through Jesus.

Acts 3 tells us that Peter and the apostle John went to the temple in Jerusalem and healed a man who had never been able to walk. This caught the attention of many people, so Peter preached another powerful sermon—this one at an area of the temple called Solomon's Porch. The sermon angered the religious leaders in Jerusalem, and they arrested Peter and John,

When a beggar asked Peter and John for money, Peter replied, "I have no money, but what I have I give you! In the name of Jesus Christ of Nazareth, get up and walk!" (Acts 3:6).

WHAT DOES THAT MEAN TO ME?

"There is no way to be saved from the punishment of sin through anyone else [but Jesus]. For there is no other name under heaven given to men by which we can be saved" (Acts 4:12).

You might hear people say that there are "many ways to God." But the Bible teaches there is only one way: through Jesus!

putting them in jail for the night. The two apostles didn't mind though, because many more people believed in Jesus because of Peter's preaching.

Peter did other great things to help the new church grow and become more powerful. Once, he traveled north to Samaria, where he taught Christians about the Holy Spirit (Acts 8:14–17). Not only that, he wrote two books that are in our Bibles today—1 and 2 Peter. In those books, he wrote about the things he had learned from Jesus.

THE CHURCH GROWS. . .AND EXPANDS (ACTS 3–8)

After God sent the Holy Spirit to Jesus' followers in Jerusalem, they performed miracles for people to see and preached the message of salvation through Christ. That first gathering of believers grew every day, and that got the attention of the religious leaders. They felt jealous because so many people were following Jesus, so they tried to stop Peter, John, and the rest of the church. When Peter and John refused to stop preaching, the religious leaders had them beaten and then sent them home.

One day, the religious leaders arrested a Christian man named Stephen, who had been accused to talking against God and the Old Testament Law. They brought Stephen in front of the whole assembly of religious leaders, but he wouldn't stop talking about Jesus. He reminded the angry religious leaders of Jewish history and the Old Testament prophets. Then he told them that they had murdered the promised Messiah, Jesus of Nazareth.

The godly Stephen, kneeling at left, is martyred—killed for his faith in Jesus—as an angry young Jew named Saul watches their coats (bottom right). Miraculously, Saul himself would soon become a follower of Jesus!

The crowd became furious with Stephen. They dragged him outside the city and threw rocks at him until he died. The Bible says that as Stephen was dying, he prayed, "Lord Jesus, receive my spirit" and "Lord, don't charge them with this sin!" (Acts 7:59, 60 NLT).

Stephen's death started a wave of opposition and violence against the Christians in Jerusalem. Because of this persecution, many Christians left the city and moved into different parts of Judea and Samaria. The Christians who stayed in Jerusalem, including the apostles, faced arrest and all sorts of bad treatment from the authorities.

One of the leaders of the persecution was a man named Saul, who was there when Stephen was killed and who "thought it was all right that Stephen was killed" (Acts 8:1). Saul spent a lot of time going to the houses of Christians in the city, arresting them and throwing them in jail because they followed Jesus.

But God had a plan even for Saul—who would later become known as Paul the apostle.

WHO SAID THAT?

See what great love the Father has for us that He would call us His children. And that is what we are. For this reason the people of the world do not know who we are because they did not know Him (1 John 3:1).

The apostle John, who was with Jesus for all of His earthly ministry, wrote these words many years after Jesus had returned to heaven. John also was with Peter during many of the events recorded in the book of Acts. John wrote the Gospel of John, plus 1, 2, and 3 John and Revelation.

AN UNLIKELY NEW FRIEND OF JESUS (ACTS 9)

The apostle Paul is a really important person in the Bible. He traveled thousands of miles over several years to tell people about Jesus and to start churches all over the known world. He wrote many letters to these churches and their leaders, thirteen of which are found in the Bible today. There is even evidence that he wrote other letters that aren't included as books of the Bible. Other than Jesus Himself, no one was more important in spreading the message of salvation throughout the world or in teaching people how to live as Christians.

But Paul didn't always love Jesus or His followers. Called Saul when he was born in a city called Tarsus, he grew up learning the Old Testament like most Jewish boys at that time. In Acts 23:6, Paul told the Jewish religious leaders that he was a Pharisee—that means he knew the Old Testament law and was very strict in following it.

As Saul's story begins in the book of Acts, he was doing everything he could to keep Christians from telling others about Jesus. When he found out that many of them had moved to a city called Damascus (in present-day Syria), he went to arrest them and bring them back to Jerusalem to be imprisoned. On his 175-mile journey to Damascus, though, another amazing miracle happened.

Right there on the road, a blinding light from heaven surrounded Saul. It was so bright that it caused him to fall to the ground, shielding his eyes. Then he heard a voice from heaven, asking him, "Saul, Saul, why are you working so hard against Me?" (Acts 9:3).

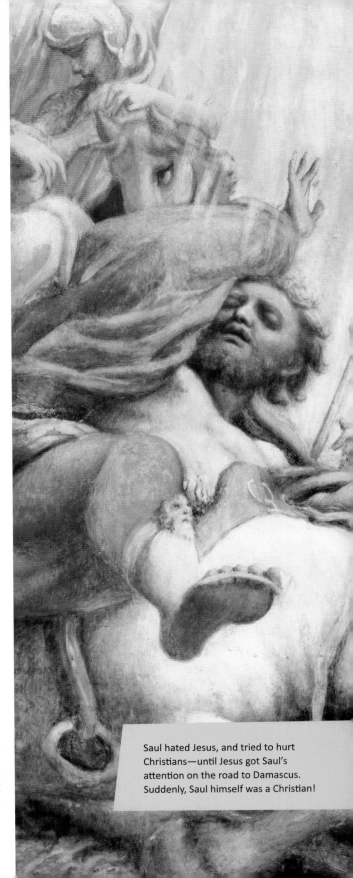

Saul hated Jesus, and tried to hurt Christians—until Jesus got Saul's attention on the road to Damascus. Suddenly, Saul himself was a Christian!

"Who are You, Lord?" the shaken and confused Saul asked.

"I am Jesus, the One Whom you are working against," the voice answered. "You hurt yourself by trying to hurt Me."

Saul knew he had no choice but to ask Jesus what He wanted. "Get up!" the Lord answered. "Go into the city and you will be told what to do."

Saul's traveling companions didn't see anyone, but they heard the voice speaking to Saul. When Saul got up from the ground, he couldn't see anything at all, so his friends led him into Damascus. Saul didn't regain his sight for three whole days.

Christians in Damascus had been worried about Saul's approach, because they knew how cruel he had been to their brothers and sisters in Christ. But one Christian man who lived in the city was prepared to *welcome* Saul into his home.

Ananias knew something about Saul the others didn't know, and he knew it because God had spoken to him in a vision. Ananias had heard all the terrible stories about Saul, and at first he didn't want to meet him. But God told Ananias that Saul had been chosen to take the message of Jesus to the non-Jewish world.

Ananias prays for Saul—a new Christian soon to be known as Paul—to regain his sight.

WHO SAID THAT?

"But Lord, many people have told me about this man. He is the reason many of Your followers in Jerusalem have had to suffer much. He came here with the right and the power from the head religious leaders to put everyone in chains who call on Your name" (Acts 9:13–14).

This was the response of a man named Ananias after God told him to welcome Saul into the church in Damascus. But God told Ananias, "Go! This man is the one I have chosen to carry My name among the people who are not Jews and to their kings and to Jews. I will show him how much he will have to suffer because of Me" (Acts 9:15–16).

God told Ananias that he would find Saul at the home of a man named Judas. (This was a common name at the time, and it is not the same Judas who had turned Jesus over to His enemies. By this time, Judas Iscariot had killed himself in sadness over his betrayal.) Ananias went, and while he was at Judas's home, he prayed for Saul to regain his sight. God answered Ananias's prayer.

Saul stayed for a while with the Christians of Damascus. They taught him more about Jesus, and before long, Saul began preaching and teaching others in the Jewish synagogue there. People were amazed that the same man who had beaten and killed people for being Christians was now preaching the message of salvation through Jesus.

Eventually, the man now known as Paul ended up in Antioch, a city in what is now the nation of Turkey. There was a big church there, and Paul helped the Christians in their faith. But then God called Paul to take a long journey to tell even more people about Jesus. God had enormous, world-changing plans for Paul—he was going to visit much of the known world, sharing the good news of Jesus and starting new churches in many cities.

PAUL'S FIRST MISSIONARY JOURNEY (ACTS 13–14)

Around AD 48, Paul and a Christian man named Barnabas set sail from Antioch. Paul's "first missionary journey" also included the young John Mark—Barnabas's nephew and the author of the Gospel of Mark. They landed first on a large island called Cyprus, where Barnabas was from. It's in the eastern Mediterranean Sea, south of modern Turkey and northwest of Israel.

The men docked at Salamis, then traveled from town to town preaching the good news of salvation through Jesus at Jewish places of worship. When they reached Paphos, a city on the western side of Cyprus, they stayed for a while. Paphos was the capital of Cyprus, and the home of the Roman governor of the island, Sergius Paulus. He was very happy to meet with Paul, and before he and his companions left Cyprus, the governor had become a Christian!

After Paul and Barnabas left Cyprus, they sailed to Asia Minor (modern-day Turkey) and landed in the area of Pamphylia. They then traveled about a hundred miles to a city called Antioch of Pisidia. By this time, John Mark had left the team and returned home to Jerusalem.

In Antioch, Paul went to the Jewish place of worship and told the people how God had brought Jesus to the world. But he also told non-Jewish people about Jesus, and many of them believed his message.

From Antioch of Pisidia, Paul and Barnabas departed for the city of Iconium, now called

SOME IMPORTANT MESSAGES FROM PAUL

The apostle Paul kept himself very busy traveling around the Mediterranean Sea, preaching the message of salvation through Jesus. But he somehow found time to write many of the books in the New Testament. Thirteen of Paul's letters (also called "epistles"), sent to churches and individual Christians, are in the Bible today. Those letters are Romans, 1 and 2 Corinthians, Galatians, Ephesians, Philippians, Colossians, 1 and 2 Thessalonians, 1 and 2 Timothy, Titus, and Philemon. Each of these letters contains instructions for living a good Christian life. They're all worth reading!

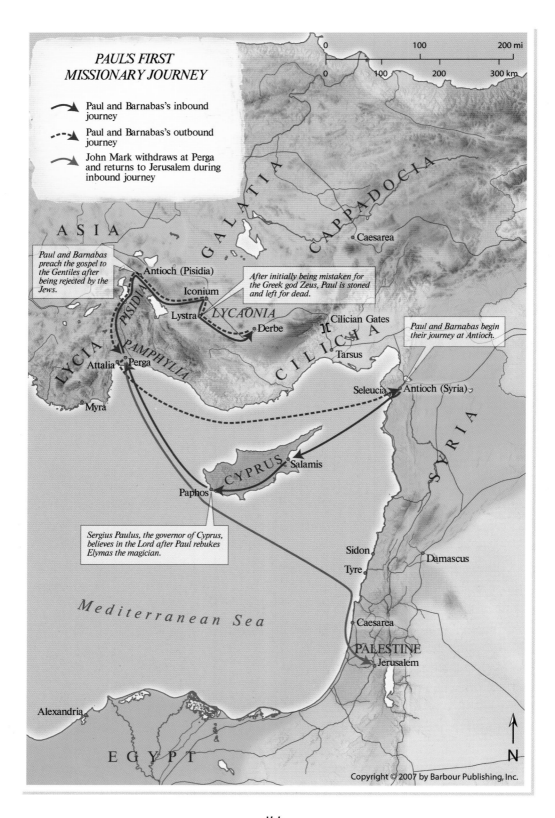

PAUL'S FIRST MISSIONARY JOURNEY

→ Paul and Barnabas's inbound journey

⇢ Paul and Barnabas's outbound journey

→ John Mark withdraws at Perga and returns to Jerusalem during inbound journey

Paul and Barnabas preach the gospel to the Gentiles after being rejected by the Jews.

After initially being mistaken for the Greek god Zeus, Paul is stoned and left for dead.

Paul and Barnabas begin their journey at Antioch.

Sergius Paulus, the governor of Cyprus, believes in the Lord after Paul rebukes Elymas the magician.

ASIA

GALATIA

CAPPADOCIA

Caesarea

Antioch (Pisidia)

Iconium

PISIDIA

Lystra

LYCAONIA

Derbe

Cilician Gates

CILICIA

Tarsus

LYCIA

PAMPHYLIA

Attalia

Perga

Myra

Seleucia

Antioch (Syria)

SYRIA

CYPRUS

Salamis

Paphos

Sidon

Damascus

Tyre

Mediterranean Sea

Caesarea

PALESTINE

Jerusalem

Alexandria

EGYPT

N

0   100   200 mi
0   100   200   300 km

Copyright © 2007 by Barbour Publishing, Inc.

Konya in Turkey. They stayed for a long time before moving on to Lycaonia, a large region in Asia Minor. In Lycaonia, they visited the cities of Lystra and Derbe. In Lystra, Paul healed a man who had never walked before.

Sadly, the people in Lystra thought Paul and Barnabas were mythical Roman gods come to earth. The people wanted to offer sacrifices to them, but Paul said that he and Barnabas were just men who had come to bring them the good news about Jesus. When Jewish people in Lystra found out what had happened, they turned the city's people against Paul and Barnabas. Before long, they were throwing rocks at Paul. Thinking he was dead, they dragged him out of the city.

Paul wasn't dead though—God still had work for him to do. So the very next day, he and Barnabas traveled to Derbe. After that, they returned to Lystra, Iconium, and Antioch. In every city, they taught and encouraged the Christians who lived there. After that, they started their trip back home.

By the time Paul and Barnabas completed their journey, they had been on the road for almost two years and traveled 1,250 miles. Along the way, they started many new churches and appointed leaders for those churches.

PAUL ON THE ROAD AGAIN (ACTS 16–18)

Around AD 50, before Paul started his second missionary journey, he and Barnabas traveled from Antioch to Jerusalem. They met with other Christians to discuss disagreements about what it took for non-Jewish people to become Christians. Some Jewish Christians believed the non-Jews needed to go through the Jewish religious ceremonies, but Paul disagreed.

At what is now called the "Council of Jerusalem," the men in attendance all agreed that non-Jewish Christians did not need to complete these ceremonies. After that, Paul and Barnabas traveled back to Antioch.

Paul wanted to take Barnabas on his second missionary journey, but they argued about whether John Mark should go with them. Remember, John had dropped out partway through the first trip. Barnabas wanted to give John Mark another chance, but Paul didn't. The issue was settled when Barnabas took John Mark to Cyprus and Paul recruited Silas, a church leader in Antioch, to travel with him in another direction.

Paul and Silas set out from Antioch, traveling through Syria and into Cilicia, which was a Roman province on the Mediterranean coast of what is now southern Turkey. Along the way, they made stops to encourage Christians in different towns. Then Paul went back to Derbe and Lystra. While there, he recruited a young Christian named Timothy to join him.

Paul's traveling party then made its way to Macedonia, another Roman province. Macedonia is now part of northern Greece, and it included cities such as Philippi, Thessalonica, and Corinth. Paul helped start churches in all three of those cities and later wrote letters ("epistles") that ended up being included in the New Testament: Philippians, 1 and 2 Thessalonians, and 1 and 2 Corinthians.

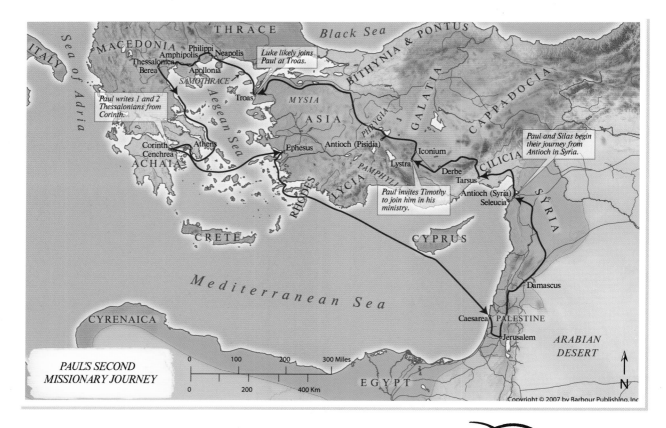

PAUL'S SECOND MISSIONARY JOURNEY

The Bible includes some great stories of Paul's visit to the city of Philippi. While he was there, a woman named Lydia became a Christian because of his preaching (Acts 16:14–15). Paul also cast out an evil spirit from a slave girl who had been making money for her master by telling people's fortunes (16:16–18). Paul and Silas ended up being beaten and thrown in jail in Philippi, but while they were there, they told the guard about Jesus. The guard and his whole family believed in Jesus and were baptized (Acts 16:19–34).

After Paul left Philippi, he visited several more cities, including Thessalonica, Berea, Athens, Corinth, and Ephesus. In Athens, Paul preached in the Areopagus, also known as "Mars' Hill."

WHO SAID THAT?

We took a ship from the city of Troas to the city of Samothracia. The next day we went to the city of Neapolis (Acts 16:11).

These words are from the pen of Luke, who wrote the third Gospel and the book of Acts. Luke was a physician and a historian. He was the only non-Jewish writer of a New Testament book. Acts 16:11 shows us that Luke actually traveled with Paul during his second missionary journey. This was the first time in telling the story that Luke used the word *we* to describe who was with Paul.

Paul and his missionary partner Silas were beaten and thrown in jail for their faithfulness in sharing the good news about Jesus. While they were being held in prison, they helped the jailer meet Jesus!

WHO SAID THAT?

"Sirs, what must I do to be saved?" (Acts 16:30).

A jailhouse guard in the city of Philippi asked Paul and Silas this important question. He was overseeing the two missionaries when an earthquake struck. The prison doors shook open, giving them an opportunity for an easy escape. The jailer figured they were gone. Knowing he would be in deep trouble with the Roman authorities if his prisoners got away, he pulled out his sword to kill himself. But Paul shouted, "Do not hurt yourself. We are all here!" The jailer had heard Paul and Silas singing and praying to God from their cell, so he asked the question above. Their answer? "Put your trust in the Lord Jesus Christ and you and your family will be saved" (Acts 16:31).

Several people believed Paul's message and became Christians (Acts 17:16–34). In Corinth, Paul met a married couple named Aquila and Priscilla, who would become important in the church in that city (Acts 18:18–21). After a short stay in Ephesus, Paul traveled back to Antioch.

Paul's second missionary trip took about three years, and it would change the world for good!

ONE LAST TRIP (ACTS 18:23–21:17)

Around AD 51, Paul started his third missionary journey. Before he went, he spent some time working with the church in Antioch. His first stop again was the regions of Galatia and Phrygia, which were located in modern-day Turkey. From there, he returned to Ephesus.

Paul had visited Ephesus during his second journey, but stayed only a short time. This visit, though, lasted almost two and a half years. He started out teaching in the Jewish places of worship, but some in the audience rejected his message and became abusive and rude. So Paul moved his teaching to a school run by a man named Tyrannus. He preached at the school every day for two years—to Jewish and Greek people alike.

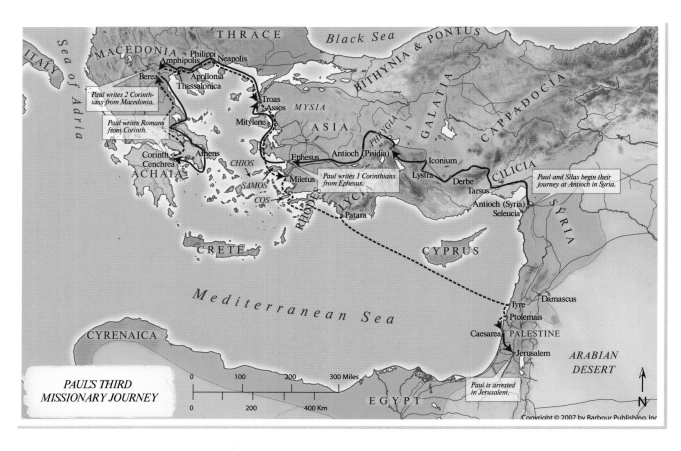

Paul writes 2 Corinthians from Macedonia.

Paul writes Romans from Corinth.

Paul writes 1 Corinthians from Ephesus.

Paul and Silas begin their journey at Antioch in Syria.

Paul is arrested in Jerusalem.

PAUL'S THIRD MISSIONARY JOURNEY

0   100   200   300 Miles

0   200   400 Km

N

Copyright © 2007 by Barbour Publishing, Inc.

God did amazing things through Paul in Ephesus. Miracles happened, people were healed, and evil spirits were cast out in Jesus' name. Paul's ministry grew so powerful that sick people would be healed of diseases and freed from evil spirits just by having cloth Paul had worn placed on their bodies!

Eventually, Paul's preaching in Ephesus got him into trouble. Many of the people who had come to faith in Jesus had been worshipers of a fake goddess called Artemis. An Ephesian silversmith named Demetrius had made a lot of money selling things related to the goddess, and he worried that if too many people switched from worshiping Artemis to Jesus, he would

lose out. So he started a riot in the city, and Paul was nearly killed. After the violence died down, Paul and his traveling companions traveled to Macedonia and then to Greece. During this time, he avoided a plot by the Jews to kill him, and he raised a young man from the dead in a place called Troas.

PAUL'S FINAL YEARS (ACTS 21–28)

Paul eventually traveled back to Jerusalem. The Christians there were happy to see him, but after seven days, some of the Jews accused Paul of doing something in the temple that was against Jewish law. Paul was dragged out of the temple and beaten. He would have died, but Roman soldiers saw the trouble and stepped in. They put Paul in chains and took him away for questioning. The Romans later sent him to a place called Caesarea Maritima, the Roman capital of Judea, where he was held prisoner for two years.

From Caesarea, Paul and his traveling companions were sent to Rome so he could stand trial before the Emperor. Paul stayed in Rome for two years. He was allowed to go where he wanted, and he lived in a home he had rented. But Roman guards were always with him to keep him from escaping. While in Rome, Paul continued to tell people about Jesus.

The book of Acts ends with Paul in custody in Rome. But when we read his letters, it appears that he was eventually released and then made other visits as a missionary. Some believe that Paul was imprisoned in Rome a second time—this time in a very rough prison—and that he wrote many of his letters as he awaited a sentence of death.

Christian tradition holds that Paul was executed around AD 67 by order of the Roman emperor Nero, who was treating Christians very badly. Nero may have persecuted Christians because he blamed them for a huge fire that broke out in the city of Rome in AD 64. Four years later, Nero committed suicide.

Paul tells the highly educated men of Athens about the "unknown God" they guessed was out there somewhere (see Acts 17:16–32).

Paul, who once approved of the death of Christians, was eventually killed for his own faith in Jesus Christ.

During Paul's second imprisonment in Rome, he wrote a farewell letter to a young pastor in Ephesus named Timothy. Paul knew that his time on this earth was short, and he said, "I have fought a good fight. I have finished the work I was to do. I have kept the faith" (2 Timothy 4:7).

Paul had done everything God had given him to do. He had preached the Gospel of salvation through Jesus in many places, and thousands of people came to faith in Christ because of it. He started many churches and also wrote to encourage and challenge them in their lives of faith.

Today, we know the message of salvation through Jesus, and we can thank Him for that. But we can also thank Paul, a man who changed the world because he loved God and did the things God had called him to do.

In the centuries after Paul and the other apostles died, the Christian faith would spread throughout the world. Millions of people came to believe in Jesus and embrace the life-changing message that He and His followers taught. That included one amazing promise Christians are still waiting to see fulfilled: Jesus, one day, will be coming back!

Boys read the Bible in Harare, Zimbabwe, Africa. More than two billion people around the world are identified as Christians, thanks in large part to the work that Jesus' apostles started two thousand years ago.

CHAPTER 10

HE'S COMING BACK!

In this book, you've read highlights of the Bible's teaching about Jesus. You've seen why He had to come to earth in the first place, as well as Old Testament prophecies about Him. You've learned about His birth, childhood, and earthly ministry. And you've read about Jesus' arrest, trial, death, and resurrection—plus the work of His followers after He returned to His Father.

It's an incredible story, isn't it? But there's still more to come. You see, Jesus' story didn't end when He ascended to heaven. And it didn't end with the work of Jesus' apostles either.

Jesus made some powerful promises when He was on earth, including this one: one day, He would return. That is the only promise Jesus hasn't fulfilled yet—but He will, and it could happen very soon.

Here is how Jesus described His return to earth: "Something special will be seen in the sky telling of the Son of Man. All nations of the earth will have sorrow. They will see the Son of Man coming in the clouds of the sky with power and shining-greatness. He will send His angels with the loud sound of a horn. They will gather God's people together from the four winds. They will come from one end of the heavens to the other" (Matthew 24:30–31).

Later on, just before Jesus was arrested, tried, and crucified, He promised His followers, "After I go and make a place for you, I will come back and take you with Me. Then you may be where I am" (John 14:3). That's a beautiful promise to everyone who has trusted Jesus for salvation.

When Jesus returns to earth, it will be with more attention than His birth in Bethlehem. Angels will announce Jesus' coming with trumpets!

Forty days after God raised Jesus from the dead, He returned to heaven. As Jesus rose up into the sky, His followers watched Him disappear from view. Just then, two angels appeared, saying, "You men of the country of Galilee, why do you stand looking up into heaven? This same Jesus Who was taken from you into heaven will return in the same way you saw Him go up into heaven" (Acts 1:11).

The New Testament includes many other promises about Jesus' return, which Christians call the "Second Coming." Here are some examples:

IT'S IN THE BIBLE!

"But you must be sorry for your sins and turn from them. You must turn to God and have your sins taken away. Then many times your soul will receive new strength from the Lord. He will send Jesus back to the world. He is the Christ Who long ago was chosen for you. But for awhile He must stay in heaven until the time when all things are made right. God said these things would happen through His holy early preachers" (Acts 3:19–21).

- "Do not be quick to say who is right or wrong. Wait until the Lord comes. He will bring into the light the things that are hidden in men's hearts. He will show why men have done these things. Every man will receive from God the thanks he should have" (1 Corinthians 4:5).
- "Christ is our life. When He comes again, you will also be with Him to share His shining-greatness" (Colossians 3:4).
- "Who is our hope or joy or crown of happiness? It is you, when you stand before our Lord Jesus Christ when He comes again. You are our pride and joy" (1 Thessalonians 2:19–20).
- "May the God of peace set you apart for Himself. May every part of you be set apart for God. May your Spirit and your soul and your body be kept complete. May you be without blame when our Lord Jesus Christ comes again" (1 Thessalonians 5:23).
- "It is the same with Christ. He gave Himself once to take away the sins of many. When He comes the second time, He will not need to give Himself again for sin. He will save all those

who are waiting for Him" (Hebrews 9:28).
- "Christian brothers, be willing to wait for the Lord to come again. Learn from the farmer. He waits for the good fruit from the earth until the early and late rains come. You must be willing to wait also. Be strong in your hearts because the Lord is coming again soon. Do not complain about each other, Christian brothers. Then you will not be judged. See! The Judge is standing at the door" (James 5:7–9).
- "See! I am coming soon. I am bringing with Me the reward I will give to everyone for what he has done. I am the First and the Last. I am the beginning and the end" (Revelation 22:12–13).

In Chapter 2 of this book, you read about some Old Testament promises of Jesus' first arrival on earth. But other prophecies predict His return. For example, Psalms 2 and 110 describe God's chosen King—Jesus—who will rule on earth. And the prophet Isaiah wrote that in the end, "Every knee will bow down before Me. And every tongue will say that I am God" (Isaiah

The first time Jesus came to earth, it was as a helpless baby. In His second coming, He'll be the all-powerful King.

45:23). The apostle Paul used very similar words in Philippians 2:10–11: "So when the name of Jesus is spoken, everyone in heaven and on earth and under the earth will bow down before Him. And every tongue will say Jesus Christ is Lord."

Jesus' return to earth is a promise from the same God who sent Him in the first place. But the Bible tells us that only the Father knows exactly when it will happen. For centuries, Christians—even those who lived in the times of Jesus' apostles like Peter, John, and Paul—have looked forward to Jesus' return. Many Bible experts have read verses like the ones above and tried to guess when He will come back. Some people have even named specific dates, but all of them have been wrong.

Some believers in the first century—that is, the first one hundred years after Jesus' birth—believed He would return in their lifetime. And some of them worried that they might miss the big event. That's why the apostle Paul wrote, "Our Lord Jesus Christ is coming again. We will be gathered together to meet Him. But we ask you, Christian brothers, do not be troubled in mind or worried by the talk you hear. Some say that the Lord has already come. People may say that I wrote this in a letter or that a spirit told them" (2 Thessalonians 2:1–2).

Jesus told His followers that only His Father knew the exact schedule: "No one knows the day or the hour. No! Not even the angels in heaven know. The Son does not know. Only the Father knows" (Matthew 24:36). But now that Jesus is in heaven with His Father, we can imagine that He knows too. We still look forward to the day, because we know that God keeps all His promises!

A woman teaches about Jesus to children in India. Missionaries obey Jesus' "great commission"—to go and teach people around the world to follow Him. When the whole world has had the chance to hear about Jesus, He will return to earth as king.

fast as lightning shines across the sky from east to west" (Matthew 24:27). The second coming will take place very quickly and that everyone on earth will know about it. The book of Revelation says, "See! He is coming in the clouds. Every eye will see Him. Even the men who killed Him will see Him. All the people on the earth will cry out in sorrow because of Him" (1:7).

Since many people are not ready to face God, Jesus' return will be a very bad and shocking surprise. To them, His return will mean judgment and eternal punishment for their sin. But for those who love and follow Jesus, it will be the day when every one of God's promises will be fulfilled. It will be the beginning of our eternity in heaven with Him!

Though we can't know the day or the hour of Jesus' return, the Bible gives clues about things that will happen before the Second Coming. First of all, Jesus said He wouldn't return until after the His Gospel message was preached to every nation in the world. Also, the apostle Paul wrote that Jesus' return would not happen until "the man of lawlessness" (who many call "the Antichrist") had been revealed. And Jesus taught that just before His return, there would be an increase in suffering and persecution against Christians throughout the world. To read about these signs, and others, look up these Bible passages: Matthew 24:4–29, 2 Thessalonians 2:1–12, and Revelation 6–18.

Jesus told His followers that His return would happen so suddenly that it would catch most people off guard: "The Son of Man will come as

IT'S IN THE BIBLE!

"For the Lord Himself will come down from heaven with a loud call. The head angel will speak with a loud voice. God's horn will give its sounds. First, those who belong to Christ will come out of their graves to meet the Lord. Then, those of us who are still living here on earth will be gathered together with them in the clouds. We will meet the Lord in the sky and be with Him forever" (1 Thessalonians 4:16–17).

This is how one artist imagines "the rapture"— as millions and millions of Christians are taken out of the world to be with Jesus.

Some people believe that part of Jesus' return is an event called "the Rapture." This is a moment when Jesus takes all living Christians, as well as the bodies of believers who had died before, off the earth to be with Him in heaven. Those who believe in the Rapture see this idea in 1 Thessalonians 4:13–18 and 1 Corinthians 15:50–54. After the Rapture, there will be terrible suffering in the world as God judges those left behind on earth. That time is called "the Tribulation."

Other Christians believe that Jesus' followers will not be removed from earth before the Tribulation. But when that terrible time is over, Jesus will come again to take believers away from all the suffering. Then He will completely destroy evil and the devil, beginning a reign of justice, peace, and righteousness on earth.

Jesus said His return to earth would come as a surprise to many people, so they should always try to be ready. "Be careful!" He said. "Watch and pray. You do not know when it will happen. . . . Watch!" (Mark 13:33, 37).

ARE YOU READY?

Jesus taught His followers how important it was for them always to be ready for His return. Since nobody knew the day or hour, Jesus told believers to keep watch at all times:

"Be ready and dressed. Have your lights burning. Be like men who are waiting for their owner to come home from a wedding supper. When he comes and knocks on the door, they will open it for him at once. Those servants are happy when their owner finds them watching when he comes. For sure, I tell you, he will be dressed and ready to care for them. He will have them seated at the table. The owner might come late at night or early in the morning.

Those servants are happy if their owner finds them watching whenever he comes. But understand this, that if the owner of a house had known when the robber was coming, he would have been watching. He would not have allowed his house to be broken into. You must be ready also. The Son of Man is coming at a time when you do not think He will come."
LUKE 12:35–40

Jesus was saying we shouldn't try to figure out when He will return. Instead, we should always live our lives as if He could return at any moment—maybe even today!

People sometimes say things like, "You

know, two thousand years ago, Jesus said He would come back to earth. And ever since then, Christians have been thinking He would come back in their lifetimes. But He hasn't. Maybe the people who wrote the Bible misunderstood what Jesus meant. Or maybe He's not coming back at all!"

One of Jesus' closest friends on earth, the apostle Peter, wrote that there would always be people who said stuff like that. But he also wrote that we should be patient when it comes to Jesus' return, knowing that our timing is not the same as God's. Besides, Peter wrote, the longer Jesus waits to come back, the more people have a chance to come to Him for salvation! (see 2 Peter 3:3–9).

Yes, two thousand years is a long time for us humans. But to God, it's like the blink of an eye.

God always keeps His promises, and one day He will keep His promise to send Jesus to earth for a second time. Until then, God wants us to live like Jesus is coming back today—not because we're afraid, but because we love Him. . .and love others enough to tell them about Him.

Jesus *is* coming back! When He does, it won't be an end but an incredible new beginning for everyone who trusts Him for salvation. The Bible says of that time, "See! God's home is with men. He will live with them. They will be His people. God Himself will be with them. He will be their God. God will take away all their tears. There will be no more death or sorrow or crying or pain. All the old things have passed away" (Revelation 21:3–4).

That's what your eternity with Jesus will look like. What an eternal life that will be!

Jesus loves children—like you! And He's eager for you to be part of His forever family!

ART CREDITS